The Adventures of
Captain Parquin

The Adventures of
Captain Parquin

The Recollections of a French
Cavalry Officer of the Chasseurs
During the Napoleonic Era

Denis Charles Parquin

LEONAUR

The Adventures of Captain Parquin: the Recollections of a French Cavalry Officer of the Chasseurs During the Napoleonic Era
by Denis Charles Parquin

Leonaur is an imprint of Oakpast Ltd

ISBN: 978-1-78282-231-8 (hardcover)
ISBN: 978-1-78282-232-5 (softcover)

http://www.leonaur.com

Publisher's Notes

Contents

Introduction

There is scarcely another topic in the whole range of literature which possesses such an interest and fascination as the extraordinary career of the first Napoleon.

Those eighteen years of his resplendent triumphs, followed by disaster almost as vivid in dramatic intensity, would appear as time rolls on to enter more and more into the realm of poetic legend. Whatever else might diminish the admiration inspired by the great emperor, is passing gently onward to the shades of oblivion, leaving only with the present a kind of reverential awe for that "man of destiny" who so long and tenaciously held sovereign sway over the fortunes of Europe.

Even amid the sternest realities of life, and where the burning race for wealth seems to be the chief task of existence, human nature still has longings for the unique, the mighty and the marvellous. The imagination requires nourishment as well as the stomach or brain, and its favourite sustenance has ever been found in the chronicles of high achievement or in the records of those dauntless men who have wielded the sword of victory on desperate fields of war. Neither fiction nor romance can claim any such hold as these on the average human mind. And, if such stirring events have been recent, if their narratives be given to us in the very words of those whom death has but lately silenced, no other possible theme can exert such a, thrilling influence on the hearts of both young and old.

This will fully explain why the reading public, in all civilized lands, has given such cordial welcome to the publication of authentic memoirs covering the period of the French Revolution and the First Empire. These narratives not only teem with the most precious historical matter, but they also shed light on the true genius of the men who gave France her prolonged dominion on the European continent—an era which has insured to its nations the survival of the better principles of the French Revolution. As distinctly personal memoirs they also display the merit, so rare in our time of being entirely free from the artifices of rhetoric, and of presenting to us the genuine, sincere impressions of eyewitnesses and actors in the great drama—features that have aroused the enthusiasm of every reader in France, and will be heartily appreciated wherever her fame and name are held dear.

The loving veneration that still enshrines the image of the "Little Corporal," remote and shadowy though it be, has always included those unconquerable French armies that made feasible and realized, during half a lifetime the stupendous enterprises of the man from Corsica. Nowadays it is clearly seen that the soldiers who looked up to Bonaparte, First Consul, and to Napoleon, Imperator, as to a being somewhat akin to the deities of the ancients, were themselves of such heroic mould that their beloved leader, having them in his wake, could well have dared to impose his haughty will on the leagued sovereigns of Europe.

Whence did these Frenchmen of the early Nineteenth Century gather their sublime energy? Were they taller or stronger than us, their descendants? Were their frames more vigorous or their hearts any braver? Certain it is that the career they embraced with alacrity at such a tender age—multitudes only in their fourteenth, fifteenth or sixteenth year—must have steeled their natures so that the comforts of civilized life held no allurement for them. In the rough school of war they must also have gained an agility surpassing that of the gymnasium, while the free air and sunshine stimulated their fighting instinct with all that this implies—keenness of perception, promptness of decision and rapidity of execution. But that which really made them invincible was rather a condition of their mental being. Reared amid the storms of the Revolution they had seen death too often and too closely to fear it at any moment, or in any form it might take. They had chosen the military life from taste and preference rather than from an impulse of obedience. They had gravitated into the army as iron glides to the magnet, not from any yearnings for honour or reward, but that simply to be a soldier, to wear a hussar's or chasseur's uniform, to go forth to the wars, to imperil their lives, to do anything and everything in the nature of wild adventure, all had for them an irresistible attraction. They had no care for the morrow, no plans for the future, no schemes for accomplishment. In some corner of France, they had doubtless beloved relatives—a father, mother, young sisters. But they rarely corresponded and always felt more at home with their regiments than elsewhere. There friendships were formed, more especially by the men who continued long in the ranks, as chivalrous and devoted as ever were those of the medieval *paladins*—friendships in which all things were shared in common, provisions and pleasures as well as sabre-strokes and gunshots; in which baseness was utterly unknown, and which, like highly-tempered swords, endured right along to the rust of inefficacy unless death stepped in on a bullet to shatter the sacred bond. Nor were these friendships less generous than powerful, for in them were seen no distinction of rank, no infirmities that were not born in partnership, nor any pretensions of intellect that rose above the common plane. Whoever has known such friendships of glowing unselfishness cannot fail to cherish their lustre as a memory of his inmost soul. Indeed all the qualities that marked the men of the First Empire, so strangely foreign to this later age, have caused many to feel incredulous of the statements of fact that have come from the lips of its veterans. Our cynical generation has always a, sneer in reserve for their marvellous narrations, which sound more like passages from an epic poem than the recitals of actual deeds by men who have fought and triumphed within this Nineteenth Century. The editor who would impress their truth on the minds of modern readers, is obliged to be extremely diligent in the study of documents and careful in the comparison of names, dates and incidents. Especially is this needful when a memoir indited by an eyewitness, himself also an actor in the great conflict, first comes to light and is submitted to the judgment of the present day. It is a case which at once compels the most thorough and critical research.

Attempts have undoubtedly been made to impose on the public memoirs of this class that were largely in the nature of piracies. On the narrative here presented—the *Memoirs of Captain Parquin*—all manner of doubt and misgiving may be instantly set aside. The editor of this admirable work has spent years of study in verifying every statement in Captain Parquin's manuscript, chiefly by its careful comparison with the records on file at the Ministry of War in Paris. Not a single name, date or event but he has fully investigated, and in every instance the veracity of the narrator has been duly confirmed. As regards the captain's personal record, or official biography, it is found to be in reality a skeleton of the published memoirs, every entry embraced in it being substantiated by letters, certificates and other indorsements obtained from his commanding officers.

The incident of Parquin's sojourn at Oedenburg, in Hungary, is mentioned in a letter of Napoleon himself, one that may be found in the official volumes of the emperor's correspondence.

But evidence more startling is likewise at hand. In the very hour when this book goes to press a witness still lives, almost in his hundredth year, who is undoubtedly the oldest survivor of that immortal army of France. This is Parquin's own friend and companion in arms, the identical Captain Soufflot who was on April 12, 1812, while fighting alongside Parquin at Mondego, captured a Portuguese standard by one of the most dashing feats of bravery that was to be inscribes in Parquin's record. This heroic remnant of the First Empire, still full of the cheeriness and vim of the 20th Chasseurs, gave a narration within the last few months to his juniors of the "Sabretache"—the leading French cavalry club—of the brilliant career of his former comrade.

But we must here give space to the complete, unabridged and unvarnished military "Record" of Charles Parquin himself, just as it has been transcribed—for insertion in this volume—from the archives of the Ministry of War at Paris. No narrative, however eloquent in diction, can rival this simple category of dates; and only Parquin's own memoirs may serve to complete without enhancing their glorious significance. The facts must speak for themselves. Before introducing the gallant captain to tell his story we shall venture to record here the few salient events of his life subsequent to the period included in these memoirs.

On the 19th of June, 1814, the Imperial Army having been somewhat reorganized by the Bourbon king, Louis XVIII, Parquin was commissioned in the 11th Regiment of Cuirassiers, and in its ranks he took part in the Battles of Quatre-Bras and Waterloo. He belonged then to Marshal Kellermann's corps, in the L'Heritier division. After the final catastrophe he passed into the light cavalry as captain in the Horse Chasseurs of the Cantal. A few years later he became implicated in a plot that was discovered among the mutinous elements of the army, and for which he was tried before the Chamber of Peers. Being asked by the chancellor why he had not revealed the guilty plans of his colonel, who was the most gravely compromised of all the conspirators, Parquin proudly replied:

"The colonel confided nothing to me; but even had he intrusted me with every detail of his plans, whatever they might be, you need not imagine that I would furnish a scrap of evidence to bring the head of an old comrade to the scaffold."

The accusation against Parquin failed for want of testimony, but

MUNICIPAL GUARD OF PARIS

MILITARY RECORD OF M. DENIS-CHARLES PARQUIN, CHIEF OF BATTALION.

Born in Paris, December 20, 1786, son of Jean Baptiste and Louise Marie.

SUCCESSIVE RANKS.	CORPS IN WHICH HE SERVED.	DATES — OF EACH PROMOTION.	DATES — OF CESSATION OF SERVICE IN EACH CORPS.	YEARS.	ARMIES.	GENERALS IN CHIEF COMMAND.	DEEDS OF BRAVERY AND SPECIAL SERVICES.	OBSERVATIONS. TITLES. DECORATIONS.
Enlisted as Volunteer	20th Regiment of Horse Chasseurs	Nivose year XI (Jan. 1, 1803)	Oct. 25, 1803	Year XII	Ocean Shore	Gen. Augereau	Wounded by a firearm and with five lance-thrusts, made a prisoner at the battle of Eylau, Feb. 8, 1807.	Made a member of the Legion of Honor April 6, 1813.
Corporal	Ibid	Oct. 25, 1803	May 1, 1804	Year XIII	Ocean Shore	Gen. Augereau		
Quartermaster	Ibid	May 1, 1806	Feb. 1, 1809	Year XIV	The Grand Army	The Emperor		
Sergeant	Ibid	Feb. 2, 1809	April 30, 1809	1806	Prussia and Poland	Marshal Augereau	Wounded in the face by a firearm at the battle of Ciudad-Rodrigo, in Spain, May 5, 1812.	
Second Lieutenant	Ibid	April 30, 1809	Feb. 27, 1813	1807 1808	Germany	Gen La Salle		
First Lieutenant	13th Horse Chasseurs	Feb. 27, 1813	Dec. 21, 1803	1809 1810	Austria	Oudinot	Wounded in the wrist by a sabre-cut at the battle of Salamanca, July 27, 1812.	
Ibid	1st Regiment Horse Chasseurs of the Guard			1811 1812	Spain and Portugal	Count d'Hrlon		
Captain	2d Regiment, ditto	March 10, 1803		1813	Saxony Prussia	Marshal Duke of Ragusa	Wounded by a bayonet-thrust at the battle of Hanau, Sept. 29, 1813. Marshal Duke of Reggio certified in writing that having been surrounded by the enemy during the battle of Leipzig he owed his rescue partly to the brave effort of M. Charles Parquin.	Made an officer in the same order June 19, 1831.
Ibid	11th Cuirassiers	Dec. 21, 1813		1814	France	The Emperor		
Ibid	Horse Chasseurs of Cantal	June 19, 1804		1815	Waterloo			
Major	Half pay	March 16, 1816					Has captured a flag from the enemy April 1812 Certificate to that effect signed by the Marshal Duke of Ragusa.	
Ibid	Gendarmes of the Bas-Rhin	Jan. 1, 1824						
Ibid	ditto of the Doubs	Sept. 18, 1830						
Ibid	Retired	Aug. 27, 1831						
Chief of Battalion, ranking as a Lieutenant Colonel	Municipal Guard of Paris	Nov. 1, 1831 / Dec. 31, 1835						

Taken off the Roster December 8, 1836.

nevertheless the War Minister pronounced dismissal from the service on the whilom captain of the Guard *chasseurs*.

Parquin, who thus lost all the benefit of his eighteen years' service and of his nine wounds, was so persecuted thereafter by the royalist police that he concluded to take refuge in Switzerland. There he met and married, in 1822, Mlle. Cochelet, the schoolmate of Queen Hortense and her old-time reader, whom the captain had encountered by chance during a brief sojourn in Holland. This distinguished lady, who has herself left behind some remarkable memoirs, was at that time the friend and companion of the exiled queen in her castle of Arenemberg. After their marriage the couple settled down on a small estate called the Wolfsberg, only a short distance away from the royal residence.

It was then that Queen Hortense, anxious to surround her son—and the probable heir to the imperial claims—with such influences as might make him worthy of his renowned uncle, invited Captain Parquin to act as military tutor to the young Louis Napoleon. When the Revolution of 1800 robbed the imperialists of their hope of a restoration in favour of Napoleon II, Parquin fell back on his original profession by re-entering the service as a major of *gendarmes*. A few years later, when his beloved prince entreated him to join in the first attempt to upset Louis Philippe's rule, and to grasp the sovereignty of France by a revolution, Parquin gladly consented to share the risks of the venture. On the failure of the enterprise the captain made this loyal and characteristic rejoinder to the assize-judge who examined him:

"Three-and-thirty years ago, as citizen and soldier, I took the oath of allegiance to Napoleon and his dynasty When the nephew of Napoleon appealed to me by that pledge I deemed it simply my duty to espouse his cause with all my heart and soul."

There we see plainly the whole man. He does not conspire—he obeys. He does not scheme in secret for a revolt—he answers the summons of his prince by hurrying with drawn sword to the aid of the desperate cause. Being ably defended by his brother, at that time President of the Paris Bar, M. Parquin was acquitted, but he once more forfeited his army rank and thenceforth had no other interest in life than to devote himself to the prince for whom he cherished such steadfast and disinterested loyalty. In 1835 his wife died, and his only child, a daughter, was taken in charge by the Grand Duchess of Baden, Stephanie de Beauharnais, who had not forgotten her affection for the mother, and caused the daughter to be educated at Mannheim with her own children.

Parquin was now reckoned among the immediate and faithful adherents of the prince, and spent his time visiting those garrisons where he was sure to meet comrades of the glorious past; and when, a few years later, Louis Napoleon landed at Boulogne in the second futile attempt to seize his hereditary rights, the captain was one of the accomplices who were captured at his side. By his side, also, he was arraigned before the House of Peers, which passed on him a sentence of twenty years close imprisonment, to be followed by police surveillance for the rest of his life—besides the customary deprivation of his rank and insignia of honour. It was a cruel penalty, but Parquin's was one of those souls whose trust never forsakes them. It was during the period of his incarceration, in the citadel of Doullens, that he indited these memoirs of such sparkling vigour and geniality of style that one may easily discern in them the robust cheerfulness for which the soldier had been ever distinguished. In truth he was a hero of such metal as no adversity could tarnish, and even though his prison bars he constantly affected to behold, near and radiant, the opening portals of the promised land.

Like the great Prophet of old Parquin was denied the joy of entering this promised land. He died on the 19th of December, 1845—which may well be regarded as a mercy in view of the imperial travesty, so unlike the empire of his dreams, that was built amid the ruins of the tottering Orléan's *regime*. What could such as he have been to the greedy courtiers who then joined in a scramble for offices and rewards? His ideal of a French Empire had been such as their debased ambitions could never comprehend. It was an ideal that had linked with imperialism all things ennobling, disinterested, chivalrous and grand. He had dreamed of a French Empire such as was utterly beyond the contrivings of Napoleon III and his followers.

Can we regret, after all, that the enthusiasts who cherish such ideals should be called away from earth ere the delusion is exposed—ere the beloved image is smirched or shattered in their very gaze? They have lived lives of sacrifice and loved the sacrifice for its own sake. They have harboured a boundless faith in the like devotion of others. Surely it is a blessing that they should descend into their graves without the heart-rending conviction that their faith and self-sacrifice were alike vain—

"*Whom the gods love best they call away soon.*"

Max Maury

CHAPTER 1

France and Prussia
1803-1807

On the 11th *Nivôse*, year XI of the French Republic—correspond-
ing to the first of January, 1803—I stepped out of the Paris diligence
at Abbeville, in Picardy, whither I had made the journey in company
with a young friend of mine, M. Fournerat. We at once began a search
for the whereabouts of M. Idoux, quartermaster of the 20th Mounted
Chasseurs, and called at that officer's address for the purpose of enlist-
ing in his regiment. The quartermaster objected to us that the muster-
roll was already full, and likewise that my friend was not up to the
standard height, nor I of the legal age to contract an enlistment. In
truth I was scarcely sixteen at the time.

"You are right, captain," answered M. Fournerat, "but will you be
so kind as to read this letter?"—handing him as he spoke a note from
Colonel Marigni, on whom we had made a call before leaving Paris.

When the quartermaster read the letter, which was simply an au-
thorization to enlist us, all impediments were promptly set aside.

Each of us was now required to deposit twenty-seven *francs* to
capitalize his regimental fund a fixed rule of the service which met
our ready compliance. Thereupon we were conducted to barracks by
a cavalryman who was on duty at the quartermaster's office, we had
asked to enter the 6th company, which was commanded by a friend

14

of my father's, Captain Lavigne, whom we saw in Paris at Colonel Marigni's house. This captain had promised my parents he would look after me in the service, and he loyally kept his word till death overtook him at the Battle of Jena, October 4th, 1806.

When we reached the barracks we found the regiment in full dress and mounted, being about to pass in review before the commissary inspector. My friend and I admired the elegance of the corps, which was considered among the very best in the army, and had only just returned from that masterly campaign of General Moreau along the Rhine. General Richepanse, whose brigade included the 1st and the 20th Chasseurs, used to say when about facing the enemy that 21 was always his winning combination.

The uniform of the regiment was striking. The headgear of the privates was a black cloth shako, graceful in form and surmounted by an orange-coloured cloth pendant: to have this pendant waving free and the red and black plume fixed on the shako was the note

of full dress. Each *chasseur* wore his hair extended to a four-inch queue, one inch at the end being bound in a black woollen ribbon, which depended an inch below the tip of the queue. Down along the cheeks hung two thick plaits of hair, weighted by small pieces of lead to hold them in place. Both the hair and the plaits were thickly pomaded and powdered white. The green-coloured pelisse had reddish-yellow facings, and was trimmed with white woollen cord; it displayed five rows of convex buttons. The trousers were in the Hungarian style and also had trimmings of white wool. Hussar boots, wrinkled at the instep, a green and reddish-yellow sash eight inches wide, with tassels of the same colours, completed the brilliant uniform. Each *chasseur* was further adorned with *mousquetaire* gloves and a sabretache that swung down two feet at the left side, being suspended by three straps to the sword-belt.

The regiment was superbly mounted. The first squadron rode black horses; the second, bays; the third, chestnuts; the fourth, the trumpeters and the musicians, were distinguished by gray horses. My friend and I felt perfectly enthusiastic, being especially carried away by the music of the band, which we thought the finest we had ever heard.

"There is only one thing that worries me," I said to my friend, "it is to have my hair cut so close on the top of the head."

"I feel about the same," he answered, "but it will grow fast enough on the back and sides, and then we'll be able to sport a queue and two side-plaits like the others." The fact is that it took upwards of a year to reach this particular goal of our ambition.

Next morning we were taken by our squad-corporal to the regimental store-rooms, where the full uniform was delivered to us. On our return into quarters the corporal whispered to Fournerat that it was customary for every fresh recruit to "pay his footing" in the squad. My friend and I each gave him a gold *louis*. The corporal thanked us effusively and from that time forward we were reckoned among the good fellows of the company. The sergeant-major of our company was a splendid looking fellow, not more than twenty or twenty-two years old; they said that he was born in the regiment, and he was certainly every inch a soldier, severe, but just. He afterward rose as high as the rank of brigadier-general. M. Lacour, which was his name, showed me much kindness and I may say that I owed to him my rapid advancement in the service.

I had been about five months in the company when one Sunday the sergeant-major, while making the preliminary inspection, stopped right in front of me and after surveying me from head to foot, said:

"Parquin, you have a fine make-up, but there's not much of the

soldier about you. Your accoutrements are clean and you handle your arms perfectly, but—have a fiercer eye, man! Stare me down! Terrify me, if you can! You are a fully-armed man."

I obeyed him on the moment in such an expressive style that he never deemed it necessary to repeat this lesson.

The corporal in charge of my room at this period was a man

named Tissé, who had received a "carbine of honour" for his bravery. With only one companion he had succeeded in rescuing three hundred French prisoners, and capturing their escort of two companies of Hungarian grenadiers.

I often had Tissé narrate to me this gallant achievement, which was graven on his carbine essentially as it is here told. He used to say to me:

"At the Battle of Hohenlinden I was detained all morning in the rear, being engaged in getting my horse shod by Robin, the company's farrier. On our way to overtake the regiment we became strayed in a forest through which we were riding, for we had no better direction to go by than the rattle and boom of the firearms at the front. On reaching one of the large clearings that are so frequent in German forests, and which supply the needed pasture for the game they shelter, we discovered, without betraying our own presence, about three hundred disarmed French infantrymen being marched away as prisoners by the *Kaiserlichs*.

"An inspiration suddenly came to us. Setting our horses at full gallop we rushed on the escort party, firing off our pistols pell-mell and shouting noisily: "'Forward!—This way! This way!—No prisoners!'

"The movement being a complete surprise, the enemy imagined they had fallen into an ambuscade, and were therefore utterly bewildered. Without giving them any time to reflect, the prisoners made a dash for their arms, recovered every gun, and in an instant the attitude of the two parties was reversed—under the leadership of Tissé and Robin the French infantry were marching the Hungarians as captives to headquarters. From that day onward the farrier was known in our regiment by the sobriquet of "Robin of the Woods."

There were several other weapons of honour given to members of this corps for special feats of bravery. Captain Lavigne had been awarded one for having, during Moreau's retreat on the Rhine, commanded the entire regiment for a day, during which time he succeeded in saving it from the most imminent peril by the dexterity of his tactics and his ferocious assaults on the enemy.

As for Captain Kirmann, who commanded the third company of the regiment, and who also wore a sword of honour, his gallantry can be described no better than by inserting the pithy statement made in writing by Colonel Lacoste, in soliciting this distinction for him from the commander-in-chief.

Here is how it was worded:

"The brave Captain Kirmann has so thoroughly worn out his sabre in actual fight with the enemy that it seems to be the duty of government to provide him with a new one."

"Granted," was the summary reply of the First Consul.

It is proper to mention here that the wearing of a sword of honour also meant double pay to its possessor.

Among the bravest *chasseurs* in the regiment was reckoned a corporal of the Élite company, who, when he was only a trumpeter, and

barely at the age of fifteen, made captive with his own hand a gigantic
Latour dragoon. When this trumpeter was out one day with the skirmishers of the regiment he rushed unawares on the dragoon in question, and shoving a pistol at his breast called out. "Prisoner, or death!"
The dragoon yielded to the threat, handed up his sword and was led
away prisoner. When the pair reached the squad which was stationed
as reserve for the sharpshooters, some of its members began chaffing
the great big prisoner—such a Hercules as he was—to let himself be

disarmed and captured by a mere boy! The Austrian gruffly retorted: "He didn't capture me; I have deserted."

"What, Henri—so he is not your prisoner after all!" was now the cry of the mischievous cavalrymen.

The sole response of Henri was to say to the dragoon: "Oh, indeed! you're not my prisoner, eh? Very well, then; mount your horse again, here are your arms; just stand off there a minute and I'll take you a second time, as once does not seem to be enough for you." On hearing this proposition the comrades of the brave boy refused to allow another fight and the disgruntled Austrian remained prisoner for good.

I got to be very friendly with Corporal Henri. He was just my own age and gave me plenty of good advice. His death took place at the Battle of Raab, in 1809, and was greatly mourned in the regiment.

Among the daredevils of the corps they always mentioned Corporal Popineau, who had been awarded a carbine of honour at L——, in the time of Moreau's famous retreat. Here are the facts:

Colonel Schwartz, of Prince Charles' army, was in command of a regiment of six hundred hussars, a corps that had the reputation of being one of the very best in the Austrian service, for it had the privilege of recruiting itself by picking the choicest cavalrymen of the whole army. Its colonel was also allowed full freedom in action. He constantly worried the rearguard of the French army, carrying off convoys, cutting into the lines, freeing prisoners, attacking on his own account whenever he found a favourable chance, and more often at night than in the daytime; in a word, he was a desperate chief of guerillas. Already he had several encounters with our regiment, and his hussars had suffered much from the bravery of Captain Kirmann. One day the colonel thought he would like to meet the captain face to face; so he managed to come up to us, protected by a flag of truce, and challenged Captain Kirmann to a duel with swords. He was told that the captain had been wounded the day before in the arm, and was just then at the ambulance. Failing to accomplish his purpose Colonel Schwartz had already turned his horse's head back to his regiment, when Corporal Popineau of the Kirmann company started after him on a gallop, and cried out:

"My captain was wounded yesterday by a shot that has disabled him for the present; I am sure he will regret deeply to miss the courtesy you offer him; but if his corporal will do in his stead I am ready to meet you on the spot."

"Your audacity just suits me," cried Colonel Schwartz, drawing

his sword. Hardly had the words been uttered when the two combatants began to manoeuvre their horses. A parry from Popineau barely came in time to save him from a lunge by the colonel, who almost at the same instant received a vigorous slash across his face.

At the beginning of year XI of the Republic, France was at peace with all Europe, though it was easy to foretell that England would not be long in breaking through the conditions of the treaty of Amiens. Accordingly the First Consul made an extended trip along the coast, and finally chose the spot, in a plain near Boulogne, where he would undertake one year later to organize a force for the invasion of Great Britain.

On the 1st of June, 1803, my regiment suddenly received orders to take the saddle, and to extend in small parties for escort duty all along the route from Amiens to Saint Valery and some distance beyond. The First Consul stopped for the night at the residence of the Mayor of Abbeville, and I was detailed as one of the dismounted squad that was to guard the person of General Bonaparte.

I can still remember with what pride and delight I stood sentinel outside the room he occupied, and how exultant I was when the First Consul, on entering the apartment, saluted me with his hand to his forehead as I brought my arms to the "present."

How far I was at that time from dreaming that ten years later I should hold the rank of captain in the emperor's personal Guard! I believe that never in all my life was there a happier or prouder moment than when I stood sentry at the door of the man who had already fascinated the gaze of Europe.

On the 1st of July, 1803, we left Abbeville for Caen, where we were to replace the 10th regiment of dragoons. This corps had of late become obnoxious to the young men of the city, who were generally of a daring and riotous character and greatly addicted to warlike exercises. Indeed there were over one hundred fencing-masters in the ancient Norman *burg*.

The 43rd Regiment of Infantry had likewise been in garrison here, but became involved in so many duels that the active enmity of the citizens compelled its retirement. In this case the Minister of War transferred the colonel of the regiment and caused a few of the offending *burghers* to be severely punished. By an order of the First Consul the 43rd regiment then went back to Caen with drums beating and colours flying. A deputation from the city welcomed it outside the gates.

Such was the condition of affairs when we arrived at Caen. Colonel Marigni, who was very fond of young people, organized a fencing tournament and invited to it as his guests all the youth of the city as well as the garrison fencing-masters. The entertainment took place in the hall of the Café Labassée, on the public promenade. An incident which was in itself of a distressing nature served to establish us in the good graces of the citizens. A sudden and dangerous conflagration broke out in one of the villages near Caen. The disaster was made known to General Laroche, commander of our division, just as he was on his way to the hall of the tournament. As he passed by the cavalry barracks where our regiment was quartered, he hurried into the guardroom shouting:

"To horse, men! To horse! There's a village on fire!"

Then turning to the guard-sergeant, he inquired:

"Where is the trumpeter on duty?"

"General, I have allowed him to go over to his squadron for supper."

"Where is his trumpet then?"

"It is hanging here with our carbines—here it is, general."

Promptly seizing the instrument General Larouche sounded the call "To horse!"

25

The notes were as promptly repeated by all the trumpeters of the regiment, and in a very few moments every man was in his saddle. The general had been a trumpeter in his youthful days and had not yet forgotten how to sound the calls. On the regiment being assembled General Larouche placed himself at its head and set off at a headlong gallop for the burning village, where our soldiers soon succeeded in saving at least all the houses that were not already in flames.

The excellent conduct of the regiment on this occasion and the brilliant fencing that took place in the evening, combined to establish us in general favour. Not only did the young citizens give us a tournament in return, but they added the gift of a splendid punchbowl in

token of their goodwill. These pleasant relations continued during the whole of our sojourn at Caen, and several youths of the best families joined our regiment as volunteers, even furnishing the entire cost of their horses and military outfit.

From Caen we removed to Rennes, where we arrived on the 10th of September and where we were to leave a depot under the command of Senior-Major Castex, a gentleman who had just joined the regiment and who, beginning as an ordinary private of the 24th Mounted Chasseurs, has since become lieutenant-general, viscount, and Grand Officer of the Legion of Honour.

On the 1st of May, 1804, Major Castex summoned me to his office and informed me that I had been named as a corporal at the request of Captain Lavigne, and that my promotion would be announced on the following day's parade, Sunday. He further told me that in my new rank I was to form part of a detachment which was about to leave for the service squadrons on duty at the ocean shore.

My company was stationed at Lannion, a very small garrison town but pleasant to live in; we left it on the 1st of December for Guingamp, and thence, on the 1st of January, 1805, proceeded to the regimental headquarters at Saint-Brieuc. We next went to Napoleonville, which we left on the 5th of April for Versailles, arriving there on May-Day. We remained at Versailles for five months, when we were ordered, October 5th, 1805, to leave for Paris. There we were given quarters at the Bellechasse barrack in the Saint-Germain district.

On the following Sunday our regiment was in the saddle for a re-view by Prince Louis, the emperor's brother. The entire Paris garrison consisted at the time of but one infantry corps, with green uniforms, called the Guard of Paris, and another regiment attired in red, also termed the Guard of Paris, but whose members the young street Arabs usually styled the "crayfishes."

Something entirely new to us was here, the Mameluke Guards. I little thought that at a later period I should have them under my command, as well as a company of the Young Guard, during the whole campaign of the invasion of France. During this review the Mamelukes dashed forward at full gallop, making no pretence of order or alignment and halting their steeds abruptly wherever they took the impulse; it was exactly like a flight of pigeons changing from one ground to alight upon another some distance away. Later on they were drilled to manoeuvre with the same regularity and observances as the other cavalry corps.

Just then the emperor was away at the head of his army and win-

ning the victory of Austerlitz. This glorious time was also an epoch of perfect tranquillity in France. Never before had there been so few troops on duty to maintain public peace; not more than three thousand men watched over Paris, and the departments scarcely contained a larger force.

Our regiment was soon to depart on foreign service. We received orders to move into Holland, where we arrived on the 1st of December, 1805. We did garrison duty at Nimeguen and next at Breda. At this time I was quartermaster of my company. The regiment had been billeted in the citizens' houses during the time needed to repair the barracks, which had been found in a wretched condition. My first billet proved very unsatisfactory and I went over to the mayor's office to ask for another; unhappily, I found it closed. I had noticed that same morning, however, in the municipal building, a lady about thirty years old who spoke French fluently and who seemed to have some authority among the officials. I inquired for her name and had her residence pointed out to me.

Mademoiselle Van V——— resided on the public square of Breda, and in addition to her duties at the mayor's office kept a small notion store. When I entered the first floor of the house I found her at dinner with two other ladies, whom I knew afterwards to be her sisters. She was so kind as to offer me a lodging room on the next floor, which had been engaged by Captain Margueron, who would not arrive for the next two weeks. It may be imagined that I was soon very comfortably settled. Mlle. Van V——— was a blonde with splendid complexion; she also had a shapely figure, and in laughing displayed two full rows of even, pearl-white teeth. She was thirty years old!—but isn't that the very age when the sex has its greatest influence over a callow youth of twenty? It is scarcely matter for surprise that I was deeply enamoured of this charming lady.

A disagreeable incident took place at that time in the regiment. Colonel Marigni had been complained of by a majority of the officers, and pending an investigation was placed under arrest in his own quarters. As he was guarded by two sentries from the 65th Regiment, commanded by his friend Colonel Coutard, it was easy for him to so arrange matters that one night he slipped out of the room, and procuring a post-chaise hurried off to Paris to seek his powerful friend, Marshal Murat, whose *aide-de-camp* he had formerly been.

Colonel Marigni was a fine looking man of about thirty to thirty-five years of age; he had a splendid appearance in his uniform and though rather feeble in tactics was a kind and considerate officer. He also had the reputation of being a brave one, but the opinion prevailed that he was more fitted for general staff duty than for the active command of a regiment. He was an expert pistol shot, was fond of high play, and whenever fortune smiled upon him was sure to treat the

regiment generously; sometimes he would even distribute, at his own expense, new gloves or plumes to every member of it. Occasionally he would suspend all punishments, too, and was therefore a supreme favourite with non-commissioned officers and men, though the regimental officers were bitterly arrayed against him and their charges set forth that he had trafficked in furloughs. Major Castex was in no way implicated in this scandal and held the command of the regiment during the colonel's absence. He gave me a new evidence of his approval of my conduct by appointing me, on the 1st of February, 1806, to be non-commissioned quartermaster of the Élite company. It may be imagined how delighted I was to receive such a promotion ere I had yet reached my twentieth birthday.

About the 10th of August we left for The Hague, the residence of the new King of Holland, Prince Louis Napoleon, brother of the emperor and the same who had reviewed us eight months before in Paris. When we arrived at The Hague the summer was at its height, and quarters were assigned to us in a beautiful park close to the royal palace. The non-commissioned officers and privates were domiciled in tents, while the officers not on duty took up their residence in the city itself.

On the 15th of August, the birthday of the emperor, we were reviewed by King Louis. Suddenly, as by one impulse, the left and right of the regiment started forward at the same time, without orders, and formed in a semicircle before the king. Six hundred voices shouted in unison:

"Long live the Emperor! Long live King Louis! Long live Colonel Marigni! We want our colonel back! We want him returned to us!"

"He shall be returned to you, my friends," answered the king.

Then the regiment fell back to its proper place in the column and we rode past at full gallop.

On the same day our bivouac was honoured by a visit from Queen Hortense. Her Majesty was seated in a barouche drawn by six horses, and had with her two ladies-in-waiting. One of these held in her hip a child of about three years: it was the little prince who was carried off by croup shortly afterward, to the great grief of the whole family and especially of the emperor. The other lady appeared to be much younger than the queen, who seemed very fond of her and often spoke to her with the kindest familiarity. I was told later that she was an old classmate of the queen, when Her Majesty was under the tuition of Madame Campan. Her name was Mlle. Cochelet, and at that time she was reader to Queen Hortense.

Captain Lavigne, who was on duty, was notified at once. He called the regiment to arms and placed the band in the centre of the line, where the queen's carriage was expected and in fact did stop. Our musicians were first-class and they at once struck up the melody so much in vogue at that time:

It was Dunois the young and brave
Was bound for Palestine—

Everybody knows that the music of this song, "*Partant pour la Syrie*," was composed by Queen Hortense herself, and on this occasion she appeared greatly touched by the delicate compliment of playing it for her. She requested as a personal favour that all punishments should he

cancelled. Captain Lavigne answered that this had been done already out of respect to the emperor's birthday.

"I hope you will at least appreciate my kind intention?" said Her Majesty to the captain commandant.

Before the carriage moved away the young lady who sat opposite the queen made a sign to Javot, our bandmaster, to come forward, and thereupon handed him twenty *louis* to be distributed in Her Majesty's name among the musicians. How crazy would my comrades have thought me if I said that afternoon to any of them: "Do you see that young lady in the queen's carriage, who is just leaning over to hand a purse to the band-master?—well, she will one day be my wife." And yet I should only have stated the actual truth. But we must not anticipate the march of time; let us go back to the regular order of my narration.

The barouche with its six horses returned with the queen to The Hague. On the same day there were a state dinner and ball at the palace. Captain Lavigne, who had been relieved from duty, was fortunate enough to be present, and even had the great honour of dancing a quadrille with Queen Hortense, who invited him through the medium of the Grand Chamberlain. It was her graceful way of thanking him for his prompt courtesy when she was driving through the camp.

On the 16th our regiment returned to its garrison at Breda, whence we departed for Cologne on the 20th of the same month.

The farewells on quitting a garrison are ever much the same—mutual regrets at parting, assurances of faithful remembrance, promises of a regular correspondence and the like. But Mlle. Van V—— further wished that I should take with me some souvenir, and having noticed that I was a smoker, she said to me:

"Charles, I want to present you that handsome pipe in the show-case on the counter, but as I cannot do it openly you must buy it from my sister, who has charge of the sales." And she slipped into my hand forty-eight *francs* for the purpose.

I confess I felt a lively pleasure at Mlle. Van V——— offering to present me with this very beautiful *meerschaum*, one which I had often been tempted to purchase if the price were not beyond my means. Nevertheless, I hesitated about accepting the gift, when the lady urged:

"What, Charles, can you object to taking a memento from your friend? That will indeed distress me greatly." Whereupon I offered no further objection and expressed my thanks as warmly as possible.

As her sister, Mlle. Henriette, was engaged with customers in the shop as I passed out, I merely saluted her, saying: "Please do not sell this handsome pipe; I intend buying it from you tomorrow. The price is forty-eight *francs*, I believe?"

"It is, quartermaster," she replied, with such a pleased expression that I thought she must be delighted at making the sale.

On entering the store at noon-time next day, I found Mlle. Henriette stationed behind her counter. She said to me: "Oh, I am so glad to see you before my sister gets back from church! Here is the pipe, and I desire to *give* it to you; I don't want payment for it! I have put the forty-eight *francs* into the cash-drawer out of my own savings."

I did not wish to agree to this; the matter was placing me in a serious dilemma. To tell Mlle. Henriette that her sister had given me money to buy the pipe would be the betrayal of a confidence; to inform the elder sister that her junior wished to present me with it would be a similar treachery. I had no other choice than to take the pipe and embrace Mlle. Henriette in token of my gratitude; though now indeed it was well that our regiment was departing from Breda, for I should have found myself in the cross-fire between two tender attachments, while the sisters must inevitably discover, each in her turn, the nature of the sentiment felt for me by the other, and thus be moved to reproaches and jealousy.

Shortly before we left Breda our regiment was ordered to cut off its queues and the two plaits of hair,—a sacrifice that vexed us all considerably. It needed the powerful reasoning of the officers, who insisted that the new style would be far tidier and more satisfactory in the field, to prevail over our discontent. Besides, Major Castex'

orders were positive, and as we were very fond of him he was readily obeyed. And this was all I got for the trouble I had taken to grow one of the finest queues and the handsomest side-plaits to be found upon the head of any private or non-commissioned officer of the 20th Chasseurs!

"Well, then," I said to my friend Henri, "since the sacrifice must be made, please take your scissors and cut these right off; I need some off my hair anyhow for a ring, and for a necklace to carry a medallion."

"Is that all?" replied Henri, laughing heartily, and he immediately performed the operation.

I had a chain and a ring made of my hair. Then I purchased a medallion and a pretty gold clasp for the necklace. For these various articles I paid a little over sixty *francs*. I was bound to prove myself even more generous than the two sisters. The day before our departure I accepted a supper tendered me by the ladies, and just as I was leaving slipped my little presents into the hands of the fair sisters.

Next morning at four o'clock the regiment passed in front of the residence of these charming sisters and I noticed a window open on the second story. Mlle. Van V——— stood there in tears and waving her handkerchief as a last farewell. I answered her *adieu* with a salute of the hand, and a few moments later this kind and affectionate lady had vanished from my gaze forever.

We left Holland by way of Nimeguen and passed up along the left bank of the Rhine as far as Cologne, where we arrived on the 1st of September and took quarters in the barracks at the village of Bruhl. After sojourning there for a fortnight the four service squadrons were organized and we resumed the march toward Mayence. On the 20th of September we crossed the Rhine and in the course of next day arrived at Frankfort.

It was a joyous surprise for the regiment, as it defiled through the main thoroughfare of Frankfort, to perceive Colonel Marigni, in the full uniform of his rank, standing beside Marshal Augereau on the balcony of the Swan Hotel. As the column approached in front of him the shouts of "Long live Colonel Marigni!" burst from its ranks and echoed along the line from the first to the last man. It was evident to the chasseurs that their colonel had been restored to them with his charges satisfactorily removed, and the fact was that Prince Murat had strongly interested himself in the case of his former *aide-de-camp*. The emperor, who was fully advised of the demonstration of the regiment on behalf of its commander at La Haye, simply replied: "A colonel who is so loved by his regiment should not be separated from it." Thereupon he cancelled the whole process of the complaint, remarking that it was all very well for officers to note the faults of their colonel, but he did not like those who played the part of informers. He then gave orders for Colonel Marigni to be present and take command of his regiment on its passage through Frankfort.

On the following day we pushed on toward the interior of Germany by Aschaffenburg and Wurtzburg. From the time when we crossed the Rhine, at Mayence, our regiment formed part of the 7th Army Corps, commanded by Marshal Augereau, whose manoeuvres were to depend on the movements of the Grand Army. A declaration of war had just been made against Prussia.

The regiment was delighted to have its colonel back, but it was no

less grieved to see Major Castex removed from the corps. The latter had received orders to report at Bonn, the little town near Cologne where the depot we had left at Bruhl was now stationed. The major was bitterly disappointed at the change, for he would have cheerfully come down one grade to continue with the army in campaign. He begged and entreated Marshal Augereau to retain him, even if only long enough to take part in the first battle. For a few days previously our regiment had been brigaded with the 7th Chasseurs, a corps which had crossed the Rhine without either colonel or major at its head. M. Castex reminded the Marshal of this fact, and obtained from him the command of the 7th until its colonel, M. de Lagrange, should rejoin his regiment. This officer did not appear during the entire campaign, and as Colonel Marigni was killed at the Battle of Jena, Major Castex, as we shall see, was promoted on the following day to be colonel of the 20th Chasseurs.

Since the passage of the Rhine we had moved forward in brigade order; the 7th and the 20th Chasseurs alternately formed the advance guard of the 7th corps, marching at the head of the column in the direction of Saxony.

It was on the 10th of October, at the passage of the river Saale, opposite the little city of Saalfeld, that our Third Army Corps, under command of Marshal Lannes, had the first encounter with a regiment of Prussian infantry, this latter being commanded by Prince Louis, nephew to the King of Prussia. These infantry could not stand the onslaught of our troops and fell back in disorder toward a ford on the Saale, where Prince Louis and a few of his escort endeavoured to make them rally. While thus engaged a sergeant of our 10th hussars, named Guindey, dashed in upon the prince with uplifted sword, crying:

"Surrender, General, or you are a dead man!"

"I—surrender? Never!" and warding off Guindey's weapon the prince made a blow with his sabre that scarred the sergeant's face, and was about to strike again when Guindey, responding by a point-thrust, pierced the prince's body and threw him out of his saddle. The escort of the prince, seeing him in personal combat with a French soldier, rushed to his assistance, and would certainly have made Guindey prisoner or killed him, if another hussar from the 10th had not come up at a gallop, shouting:

"Keep on, sergeant," and firing a pistol he stretched a Prussian trooper dead. That served to scare off the prince's escort, which rode back in disorder.

The death of Prince Louis of Prussia, when published throughout the French Army, gave rise to the following squib, which sufficiently proves that a battlefield does not always beget doleful sentiments;

It was Prince Louis Ferdinand,
Who thought his prowess none could stand—
The silly wight!
A French hussar just crossed his way,
And cried: "Hold on, young man, I pray,
"You talk too big;
"And on my word, with this good sword
"I'll stop your jig!"

Wounded as he was Sergeant Guindey could not hope to maintain his ground with only one hussar to assist him; he therefore escaped with the latter to a reserve squadron that was supporting our sharp-shooters. On reaching it he said to the officer in command:

"Lieutenant, if you will hurry with me as far as the river, scarcely a thousand yards away, we can find the body of a general whom I have just killed; he is the one that gave me this slash in the countenance, and we can get his sword and decorations before the enemy recovers them."

The officer and his squadron started off with the sergeant at high speed, and on reaching the spot found two hussars of the 9th, which was brigaded with the 10th, hovering round the general's remains.

"It was I who killed him," exclaimed Guindey; "my sword-blade is still red with his blood and his body must show a stab right through the chest. You may keep his purse, if you have found one—I yield it to you; but I demand his sword and decorations to bring them to the marshal myself."

The hussars of the 9th Regiment gave to Guindey the articles he justly claimed and he straightway went with them to the marshal. Just as he reached him some Prussian prisoners, belonging to the 3rd corps of the enemy, were announcing that Prince Louis of Prussia, their general-in-chief, had been killed but a few moments ago by a French hussar. This piece of news was too important for the marshal not to convey to the emperor at once. Guiney had gone to the ambulance to get his wound attended to, so he could not be sent himself as the marshal's envoy to headquarters. The sabre and decorations of the prince were accordingly despatched by one of the marshal's own *aides-de-camp*. The emperor made Guindey a knight of the Legion of Honour, and remarked: "I would even have made him an officer if he brought me the prince alive."

When the marshal, on the morning of the 12th of October, before leaving Saalfeld, went to see Guindey at the ambulance and bring him his cross, he did not fail to repeat to him the remark of His Imperial Majesty in granting the decoration.

"It was not my fault, marshal; you can see what a slash he gave me," was the reply of Guindey as he pointed to his wounded face, and added: "I can assure you that the prince had no idea of surrendering."

On the eve of the Battle of Jena, October 13th, 1806, our regiment, along with the whole 7th Army Corps, was obliged to make forced marches to reach the position assigned to it. We bivouacked that day in the fields adjoining a village where the marshal and his staff were quartered, and where there was also a division of infantry commanded by General Desjardins. This division was to occupy, and did so most effectually, an important defile through which our army corps must advance next day to reach the battlefield of Jena, where the entire Prussian Army was now concentrated.

Being close to the village of Gera we were well supplied with meat,—the mutton and goose that so abound in Saxony. The place of our bivouac was a potato-field, where we had merely to stoop to dig up plenty of potatoes, an operation which we performed with new-pattern bayonets that had just been issued to us and were destined to no further service in our hands. In fact we left them every one in the

potato-field, and were charged seven and a half *francs* apiece for them at the end of the campaign, though this weighed as nothing against ridding ourselves of an awkward and useless weapon.

On the 14th of October, 1803, at break of day, which at this season of the year comes tardily, the first division of the 7th Army Corps advanced against the position we had been ordered to occupy. The ground was vigorously defended by the enemy. That defile was to be captured; so we were under arms at seven in the morning and our cavalry division moved forward under command of General Durosnel, afterwards *aide-de camp* to the emperor and governor of the Corps of Pages.

The way was already strewn with dead bodies.

"They've been ripping things round here," said our *chasseurs* one to another. I took advantage of a brief halt to ride over to my old captain and wish him good morning. Captain Lavigne received me cordially and passed me over a drink which I accepted with pleasure. The cannon were already thundering in fierce and prolonged chorus, kindling that feverish thrill which all soldiers have experienced. I began to show some impatience that we were not sent forward at once.

"Don't worry, Parquin," said Captain Lavigne to me," they may begin the game without us but will certainly not finish it; there will be play enough in it for us all."

Our column having resumed its march I took my leave of the captain. Alas! I was never again to hear his kindly voice.

When we passed through the end of the defile into the plain, Colonel Marigni, whom we met at the opening, and who by voice and gesture was urging his *chasseurs* to a livelier pace—we were riding in column of fours—addressed me the question:

"Quartermaster, have you a good horse?"

"I have, colonel," I answered.

"Well, I wish you to remain near me; you will do duty as my orderly all day."

His adjutant, M. Isnard, had just then been struck down by a cannon-ball, so I remained near my colonel while feeling quite proud of this new distinction. I was still under twenty years of age and had been nearly four in the army; this was the first time I found myself in face of the enemy, and I was nobly ambitious to make a high record; therefore I was most fortunate to begin under the eyes of my commander.

When the Élite company had entered on the plateau from the defile, the colonel ordered Captain Fleury, who commanded it, to form up at the left of the 7th Chasseurs; then he said to me:

"Quartermaster, you stay close to the defile; and as soon as Captain Sabinet of the fifth company comes out, order him to trot to the left of the Élite, and give the same order to each company successively; then rejoin me as fast as your horse can carry you. I shall be in front of the centre of my regiment."

The colonel started, and I accomplished my mission. While I was engaged in it, a number of the wounded passed me on their way toward the ambulance. I shall never forget a sergeant of the 5th Hussars, with a most martial face, whose white pelisse was dangling from his shoulder all sodden with blood. He had just had his arm shattered by a ball and yet cried out incessantly to the *chasseurs* who passed him in emerging from the defile:

"Push on, brave *chasseurs*, push on! Those Prussians are just your game."

When the seventh company, which was the last of the regiment, had come out of the defile, I hastened at a gallop to rejoin the colonel, who was at that moment giving the order for cloaks to be folded and strapped across. The colonel appeared proud and happy to see his regiment of six hundred *chasseurs* drawn up in battle array, every man of them determined to do himself credit in the conflict. The weather was splendid; the sluggish mists of the morning had all cleared away; it was eleven o'clock; the whole sweep of the plain was afire with the belching of cannon and musketry, while a prodigious number of hares, for which Saxony is famous, were scampering hither and thither across the vacant space, their terror being hailed with a laugh by the waiting cavalrymen. An occasional cannonball plunged as far as our ranks, but this was such a trifle as to command no attention.

Suddenly an *aide-de-camp* from General Durosnel galloped up to our colonel and spoke a few words to him. In a moment our commander turned to a private who was in attendance on him and ordered:

"Dismount, *chasseur*, my saddle appears to be slipping; tighten up

the girth a bit; we are going to charge.'" The *chasseur* sprang to the ground and shoving an arm through his horse's bridle took hold between his teeth of the colonel's saddle girth, the officer moving forward his left leg to facilitate the tightening. At that very moment our poor colonel was struck by a cannonball which took off his head.

The colonel's horse, no longer feeling the guidance or control of

a hand, started away in terror and escaped in the direction of the enemy. The *chasseur* made haste to remount his horse, while I galloped back to my place in the Élite company, but not before reporting to Major-Commandant Watrin the fatal mishap that had deprived us of our colonel.

" I saw him fall," was the commandant's reply to me.

Ten minutes passed away before the regiment received any orders. This was a grave misfortune, in the first place for ourselves, who had to endure thus long the enemy's cannonade, and also for the 7th Regiment of Chasseurs, which had pierced the Prussian Army through the first and second lines, but then finding itself without support from the 20th Chasseurs, had to forego all the benefit of one of the most brilliant charges that took place during the day.

When General Durosnel at length gave an order it was for our regiment to fall back out of range of the enemy's fire, the movement being promptly made at the trot in column of fours.

I had the grief to see Captain Lavigne struck dead before my eyes—the same officer who had quieted my impatience in the morning by saying: "Parquin, there will be game enough for us all." I felt sincere regret at his loss.

During the entire day our brigade was moved hither and thither under the Prussian fire, which inflicted much damage on us, but the 20th Chasseurs never dealt a sabre-stroke and the 7th only made one charge which proved barren of result. In our army corps at least it was the infantry and artillery that bore off the honours of the day. I can still behold the 16th and the 7th Light Infantry, the 14th and 27th of the line, crashing into the enemy's columns in spite of the deadly hail of musketry and grape-shot; the fifes that rang shrill from their bands did not fail in a single note, the gaps that were ploughed in their ranks were filled as the balls swept through, and wherever those heroes advanced with their bayonets "fixed" the Prussian artillery and infantry had to surrender at discretion.

One column of captured Prussians, with its musicians at the front, was defiling just before our regiment when its bandmaster was recognized by the *chasseurs*, notwithstanding that he took some pains to avert his countenance. "It is Javot!" they exclaimed. And in truth it was the same Javot that had formerly been bandmaster to the 20th Chasseurs. He was a skilled musician, and in addition to some merit as a composer was a splendid player on the cornet. When Colonel Marigni left the regiment temporarily in Holland, Javot, to whom the colonel was personally a source of income, concluded to depart himself and turn his talents to account in Prussia. He accordingly went to Berlin, where a Prussian colonel offered him such inducements that he took service in the regiment which was here made captive in a body. On returning from his charge at the head of the 7th Chasseurs, Major Castex took the chieftancy of the 20th, which its colonel's death had vacated, and

immediately had Javot turned over to his command. Our dead were so numerous that it became easy to find a uniform to fit the bandmaster, and at the head of the 20th Chasseurs Javot made his entry into Berlin just a week after he was made prisoner, and only three weeks from the day he left it at the head of the Prussian regiment.

On the evening of the battle we bivouacked in the suburbs of the city of Weimar, where I spent a sad night, for I had made a visit to Lieutenant Lavigne, who was mourning the death of his beloved brother.

Next day I had to go out in a foray to procure some victuals from a neighbouring village. When I returned at night I was greatly surprised to learn, by one of the emperor's bulletins which reached our bivouac quite late, that on the previous day we had won a mighty battle: fifty thousand Prussians had been killed or taken prisoners three hundred cannon and sixty standards were captured. I must acknowledge that I, had no idea the victory was so great. Our regiment had indeed lost a number of men from the enemy's fire, but it had made no charge, nor even dealt a sabre-stroke, nor had we captured a single prisoner of the immense host.

"The other regiments must have done better work than we did," I could not help complaining to Henri on the subject.

" Don't worry," he replied, "our turn will come some day."

The whole army was not collected around Jena; the cavalry of the Guard had not yet arrived, while the 1st Hussars were on duty near the person of the emperor. It was only on the evening of the same day that Prince Murat reached headquarters with the "white waistcoats," as the army used to call the *cuirassiers*; his brave troops had contributed very much to the success of the battle by relentlessly pursuing the enemy who were already in full retreat when his division reached the fighting ground.

We remained three days in bivouac to recuperate and to brush up our accoutrements; all needed it badly. During these three days, to everybody's great satisfaction, Major Castex was formally commissioned as our colonel. At last, on the 18th of October, we set out on the march again, forming the vanguard of the 7th corps; on the 25th we reached the vicinity of Berlin, having advanced in regular stages without meeting even a sharpshooter of the enemy.

We spent the morning of the 25th near the gates of Berlin, so as to allow Marshal Davoust's corps the honour of entering the city first; a distinction due to it on account of its splendid behaviour at the Battle of Auerstadt.

53

Our brigade followed behind the 3rd corps and entered Berlin at two o'clock in the afternoon. It was a beautiful autumn day; the city looked very elegant, but sad; all the shops were closed, nobody was gazing out of the windows, and there were very few people on the streets; no carriages were abroad, and the only noise to be heard in the thoroughfares was that made by the artillery and ammunition-wagons of our army. We merely crossed the city to occupy a number of villages some miles beyond Berlin. The infantry of our army was quartered in the capital itself.

In the village which we occupied the country-folk had deserted their homes; we found in them plenty of forage for our horses, the harvest season being just over, but of provisions such as meat, bread, beer

and cognac, our needs were to be met by the municipality of Berlin.

Next day after our arrival the trumpets sounded the quartermasters' call; it was to go to Berlin and draw four days' rations of food, of which we were short. Having procured a number of wagons we set out for the city, the quartermasters and fatigue men being all under command of Adjutant Mozer. When our regiment had marched through the city it was silent and sad-looking; this very next day its aspect was quite the reverse—positively it might he likened to a junior Paris. the citizens were moving gaily to and fro about their business, and Adjutant Mozer concluded he would take a stroll to himself for pastime. Accordingly he came up to me, just as we were entering the city, and said: "Quartermaster of the Élite company, this issue of ra-

tions will last for three hours, and it is now only noon. You will command the detachment on to the storehouse; there you may have the
men and horses refreshed and when your turn comes round you will
draw the supplies. Here are the warrants for them and the detail of
what is to be distributed to each company and the regimental staff.
In short, you will take my place in all particulars; I am going to have
dinner at the Black Eagle."

"All right, adjutant," was my reply.

I led my detachment over to the storehouse, and had been waiting there about an hour for my turn when an orderly approached me with a letter for Adjutant Mozer. As I was acting in his stead I opened the despatch. It was an order to receive no supplies, to tear up the warrants, and to join the corps as fast as possible with the quartermasters, as the regiment had already started in the direction of Neustadt. I at

once gave the signal to mount, and sent the same messenger over to the Black Eagle to notify Adjutant Mozer that I was on my way to the regiment with the other quartermasters.

Just as I was about tearing the warrants, a Jew who had been in charge of the distribution came to me, and said:

"Quartermaster, is the adjutant who held the warrants for your supplies in the neighbourhood?"

"No," I answered him, "but I am here in his stead."

"So you have the warrants, have you?"

"Yes, of course I have them."

"Now that they are of no use to you, since you receive no supplies, what are you going to do with them?"

"That is a funny question! I am going to tear them up of course."

Then the little Jew came closer to me and whispered: "Mr. Quartermaster, why don't you do as the adjutant of the 7th has done? Won't you come to some similar arrangement with me?"

"What do you mean? I asked him.

"Well, he gave me his warrants in return for one hundred gold *frederics.*"

"How do I know you are telling me the truth?"

The only answer the Jew made was to show me the warrants drawn in favour of the 7th regiment. Satisfied that he had stated a fact, I thought there was no reason why I should not follow suit, so I handed over to him the warrants and in exchange received one hundred gold *frederics*, each of them value for about twenty-one *francs*. The detachment being now on horseback we marched off at once, following the route the colonel had prescribed in his letter. We had been on the road for two hours when Adjutant Mozer joined us. He rode up to me at once, and asked with great concern what had become of the warrants, since there had been no distribution.

"I am afraid you will scold me, adjutant, but here are fifty gold *frederics* that I accepted in exchange for them."

"That was not clever of you," retorted the adjutant, pocketing the money, "you might have obtained more for them."

I had done well to take my share in advance from a gentleman of such strict principles, for the adjutant never thought well to offer me a single *frederic*. Meanwhile I was quite delighted to be rid of all responsibility and at the same time have my belt-pouch tolerably well lined. The following day we arrived at Neustadt, where the regiment had already come to a halt and bivouacked outside the town. A canal alongside the Oder, which river flanked our bivouac on the left, contained a throng of boats heavily laden with merchandise that had evidently come from Berlin, the capital being only fourteen miles distant from Neustadt.

The morning after I joined the company I met my friend Henri, and showing him my belt told him that he could make free with its contents.

"Many thanks," answered Henri, "but the Prussians have already supplied me with all I need."

"Is that so?"

"Yes, just feel my belt."

Mine was nothing compared with his. I asked him at once, with much astonishment, what could have been the source of his luck. Henri insisted on my story first, and when I had told it, he said to me:

"You are a downright simpleton, else you would have twice the amount you have. What need had you to give the adjutant those fifty *frederics?* You had merely to say to him, 'I tore up the warrants.' He wouldn't have gone back to Berlin to find out the truth. Now here is my story; I also got my money out of a Jew; but I did not have to give him any warrants for it; all I had to do was to close my eyes, and as the affair happened in the middle of the night, and I am very fond of a nap, that was not a hard thing to do. It happened while I was on guard at the outposts. A little Jew came up and requested me, in the most polite way imaginable, to be kind enough not to notice him while he opened the canal locks to allow his boat, which was the first in line, to go on its way. I had not been instructed to look after the boats, having received no other orders than to place my sentry in the daytime on top of the hill, a thousand feet from the canal, and at night half-way up the hill. So I allowed myself to be moved by the Jew's entreaties, and permitted the first boat, which he owned, to go its way unhindered, while he slipped into my hand two hundred *frederics.* As it all happened in the dark I should like to know who could be the "wiser?"

I congratulated Henri upon the lucky night he had passed.

"Five days from now," resumed my friend, "I shall be again on duty at the bank of that delightful canal; and if I have no further orders, and the Jew should return, I expect we shall make a similar bargain. Those are the kind of chances, my dear fellow, that a *chasseur* may expect during campaign. We style them plucking a chicken's feathers without raising a cackle."

We remained a whole week in the bivouac, and our men must have made good use of these seven days, for the regiment had soon more *frederics* in its pockets than it knew what to do with.

Immediately before our departure all the boats that remained in the canal vanished in one night, and the rumour spread about that sixty thousand *francs* had changed hands as the price of their exit. Of course such a sum was not paid either to privates or non-commissioned officers; it was too big a haul to reach down to the rank and file of the regiment.

When the campaign of Prussia had ended at Tilsit, Colonel Castex in his order of the day used the following significant words:

"*Chasseurs*, I know that you have plenty of gold in your possession; whether you got it rightly or not it is yours now, keep it; but remember that you can get no more by the same means, because of the peace that has just been signed."

We marched toward Posen, which we reached on the 25th of November, and there crossed the frontier on our way to Warsaw. We were now advancing against the Russians, not against the Prussians.

We rested for two weeks in a village about ten leagues from Warsaw. The army was billeted on the people all over poor Poland, but our regiment was supplied with plenty of money and kept the inns constantly filled.

In one of these hostelries owned by a Jew, a quarrel arose on the most trifling pretext between the hussars of the 8th and the *chasseurs* of my regiment. I happened to be present. A corporal of the Élite company called Popineau, who was chief fencing-master of our regiment, raised his voice and demanded, so as to put a stop to the contention, if there were present in the room a fencing-master among the hussars of the 8th. A sergeant trumpeter, decorated with the cross of the Legion, stood up at once, and declared himself to be the foremost fencing-master of the 8th Regiment of Hussars. All quarrelling ceased at once. Corporal Popineau motioned me to follow him, and as I was stepping by his side, he said to me:

"This is an affair between regiments; I have entire faith in you, quartermaster—should I fall, you will not let our regiment be disgraced."

"You may depend on me," I returned, and seizing a lantern, the trumpeter's second and myself lighted up the way.

We found a convenient spot on a meadow behind the house. The affair was urgent, as the 8th Hussars were only passing through the village and were to start at break of day to join their army corps.

The preliminaries were short; we simply measured the weapons, which were of course the same length as they were of the same issue. Each of the adversaries held his sabre with the keen edge uppermost; they did not use them, however, as sabres, but as fencing foils, and it was easy to see that practiced masters of sword-play were pitted against each other. After several thrusts, parried in good time, Popineau missed one move and, although wounded but slightly, was so disabled as to be out of the fight. I immediately pulled off my coat and asked permission to take a hand in the game. Popineau now held the lantern, for he still had strength enough to render us this trifling service.

I had paid close attention to the method of the sergeant-trumpeter while he was fencing against Popineau. He was left-handed, and with an adversary of that kind it is always prudent to take the inside track. We had not been facing each other more than a couple of minutes before I made an outside feint, and rapidly sweeping my sword inward touched him in the left breast. The trumpeter fell, and for a few moments we were in a terrible fright lest his wound should he mortal. Happily, it did not prove to be quite so bad. When we told him to cough he was able to do so without feeling any pain; although it caused the blood to flow more abundantly. The regimental surgeon, whom somebody had quickly called, came over to the inn and attended to both the wounded men. Of course the trumpeter of the 8th could not march next morning with his flag, but had to remain with us. We took excellent care of him and when our regiment resumed its forward way he accompanied us as far as Warsaw, where he arrived on the 10th of December, and from thence set out to rejoin his own command. I met him several years later when both he and I were in the *chasseurs* of the Imperial Guard.

On the 6th of December we crossed the Vistula near Warsaw, but did not meet the enemy—I mean the Russians—until we reached the ford called the Boug, where our Mamelukes, on the 24th of December, had a brisk encounter with them. The costumes of these horsemen occasioned much surprise, not unmixed with terror, to the Rus-

sian troops, who imagined them to be Turks. The Mamelukes in their brilliant charge carried off twelve cannon, which had been set up in battery and were causing great embarrassment during the deploy of our columns. After our passage of the river—an operation which took much time and occasioned us many losses—the enemy gave way and we occupied the Polish villages, where we were received like brothers by the people, miserably poor though they were. In Poland, as in Russia, there is in each village a house of some pretensions which is called "the *château*," being the residence of the local proprietor of the soil. About that time our horses were getting a sufficiency of fodder, and we were furnished with bread—though very black of colour—

cow-beef and some beer. Cognac was quite scarce and we had to pay it with the Prussians' money. We camped there for five weeks, deriving great benefit from the rest, while our horses likewise throve wonderfully. The season was the depth of winter.

On the 1st of February, 1807, we left our cantonments, and the emperor, who had remained at Warsaw with his Guard and the army corps of Marshal Davoust, again crossed the Vistula and pushed forward with his entire army.

On the 6th, in the morning, I was one of the volunteer skirmishers sent out by Colonel Castex in advance of our regiment, when I came very near being the victim of my own bravado and eagerness to get acquainted withi the Cossacks, then seen by me for the first

time. I galloped out alone over the snow-covered plain, pistol in hand, toward a group of Cossacks, and on reaching about ten paces from them fired; I saw one of the Russians fall. So far all was well, but as the party dashed after me I turned round too short and my horse fell down in the snow. At this critical moment I should have been either killed or captured were it not for my self-possession. I dragged myself quickly from under the horse, which at once sprang to its feet again, and then passing my arm through the bridle took a pistol in each hand, ready primed, and aimed them both at the Cossack who was nearest to me. This had the effect of keeping him at a respectful distance long enough, fortunately, for an officer of the 3rd Hussars—a M. de Beaumetz, who was then seeking for his regiment—to come to my assistance. His intervention gave me time to mount my horse again. In a twinkling I was galloping off to safety, but was minus my plumed shako which had fallen in the snow. On reaching our line of skirmishers I cried out to the Cossacks to restore my shako—which they were waving exultantly from a lance-head—and offered to pay them for it. To this they signalled acceptance and I threw them a gold *frederic*. It was a costly bargain to me, but after all it was my Berlin Jew who was paying for the fun.

The outcome of this incident was a friendship which I contracted for the Count de Beaumetz, whom I met later in one of my garrisons in Spain and again in the Imperial Guard. He was the son of a member of the old Constituent Assembly, and, on inheriting a large fortune quitted the army in 1823, being then lieutenant-colonel of a regiment of hussars, every member of which was grieved at his retirement. But we must return to the incidents of our march against the enemy.

The fight at Mohrungen, where the Russians attacked us and were repulsed, as the beginning of this terrible resumption of hostilities. The skirmishes of Bergfried, Waldorf and Deppen, were all preludes to the Battle of Eylau. At that time our brigade formed the advance guard of the 7th Army Corps, which fought during the whole day of February 7th and carried the cemetery of the city of Eylau and its famous plateau. The 14th Regiment of Infantry of the line suffered terrible losses that day; forty-four of its officers were buried in one grave at the cemetery in the evening.

With the exception of some cannon-shot that reached into our ranks, killing a few of the men, our regimental loss was but trifling as compared with the awful hecatomb sacrificed in the corps of Marshal Augereau.

As it seemed unlikely that we should find forage for our horses in Eylau, now in occupation by the marshal. General Durosnel obtained permission to remove the cavalry bivouac about half a league beyond the city, to the left, where two farms had been discovered that were well supplied with provender.

There we managed to obtain abundant fodder for the horses, but no victuals could be found for the men except a few potatoes and some rancid pork.

The ground on which we made our bivouac had been disputed with our troops, by the Russians, inch by inch, and they had there lost a considerable number of men. Indeed this campaign had become so desperate that our soldiers used to say: "It's not enough to kill a Russian; you must push him before he will fall."

I remember how during that evening, when shovelling away some snow to clear space for a fire, made with the fragments of the barn-doors, we had to remove likewise a number of dead bodies; and the same night when I flung myself down to sleep, one of those corpses covered with straw served me as a pillow! I slept quite soundly.

At dawn of the next day, February 8th, the brigade had just mounted and set off towards the city, the general being at its head, when Marshal Soult sent an *aide-de-camp* to General Durosnel with orders not to leave his position but to draw up the corps for battle and await further instructions.

A little later on Marshal Soult ordered our brigade to the front of the artillery park of the 4th corps. My own regiment was formed up for action, being supported on the right by a battalion of the 27th Infantry, massed in square, and as a rear line by the 7th Regiment of Chasseurs. During the whole morning we were under fire from the enemy's artillery, though their aim was so bad that but few of the balls reached us. The hottest of the battle was at the right and in the centre. The weather was not too cold, but there was a tedious heavy snow-fall which the north wind blew straight into our faces with almost blinding effect. The pine forests that abound in this country, and which loomed up darkly as a frame to the battlefield, gave to it an additional aspect of dreariness. The leaden clouds, so low that they seemed to be upheld by the tree-tops, draped in the scene as with a funeral pall—only serving the more to remind us how very far away we were, more than three hundred leagues, from the sunny skies of our beloved France.

About two o'clock in the afternoon an immense force of cavalry

moved forward against us, but only at a walk, as the snow and the marshy soil admitted of no quicker pace. The troopers were filling the air with hurrahs, to which some of our *chasseurs* responded by shouting "*Au chat*," which means "to the cat," since *hurrah* sounds to a Frenchman as if one said "to the rat." The joke quickly spread along the whole length of the regiment.

Colonel Castex now inquired if our carbines were loaded. On receiving an affirmative answer he gave the order "Carbines, ready!"—as in campaigning we had the practice of carrying those weapons at the hooks. He next ordered the officers to fall into place in the column and then did so himself.

Meanwhile the huge mass of dragoons was steadily approaching us, still at a walk.

Colonel Castex regarding them perfectly unmoved. Only when the Russians had approached within six paces of us did his voice ring out sharply: "Fire!"

The command was carried out by our regiment as steadily as if on parade. The effect of this one volley was terrific—almost the entire front rank of the Russian dragoons was mowed down. But scarcely a single moment did the enemy waver, for almost immediately the second line took the place of the dead and wounded and the conflict became general. Were it not for Captain Kirmann's presence of mind our regiment would now lie in the greatest peril, for a swarm of Cossacks rushed against our left flank so as to place us between two fires. To his own command the captain promptly ordered: "Squadron, to the left, wheel!" and thus defeated the enemy's plan. At length the Russian cavalry column, although double ours in number, realised its total failure to cut into our ranks and was forced to turn bridle without inflicting serious damage. Nevertheless more than one hundred men of the 20th Chasseurs were either killed or wounded. The Russians suffered a loss of at least three hundred men, for the square of the 27th Infantry poured in on them a damaging fire as they were slowly falling back.

The emperor had taken position on a hill from which he could survey the whole battlefield. His eagle eye lost not a single detail of our fighting. He observed early the critical condition of the artillery of the 4th Army Corps, and showed great satisfaction when he saw the Russian cavalry repulsed and sabred back in complete disorder. He immediately sent one of his *aides-de-camp* to compliment the 20th Chasseurs, this messenger being welcomed to our ranks by thunderous cries of "Long live the Emperor!" while our *chasseurs* waved high their sabres still reddened with the blood of the Russian cavalrymen.

About four o'clock in the afternoon we heard the booming of artillery at our left. It was Marshal Ney who was coming into line with the 6th Army Corps, driving before him the Prussian regiments—commanded by General Lestock—which had formed the extreme right of the enemy's army, and only came up in time to be witnesses of the disaster of the day.

The 8th, the Battle of Eylau, was a glorious day for the entire army, and the 20th Mounted Chasseurs had seized with enthusiasm this chance to atone for its unwilling inaction on the field of Jena.

The *aide-de-camp* whom General Durosnel sent to Marshal Augereau, found the latter, on his arrival, in a wounded condition. The marshal hurried him forward to make a statement to the major-general of Marshal Soult's error in holding back his brigade from the corps in action. Prince Berthier, who was major-general, merely replied to the *aide-de-camp* "That's all right."

Then he added: "Captain, you will remain for an hour or two with my general staff; I may need your services."

It was then almost three o'clock. Captain Lafitte, which was the name of this *aide-de-camp*, and whom I well knew afterwards as a major in the *chasseurs* of the Guard, has often narrated to me what he witnessed in Prince Berthier's headquarters during that 8th day of February at Eylau. I shall tell the story in his own words:

A rumour had reached the headquarters of the Prince of Neufchatel that the Russian army, which since the 1st of February, 1807, when hostilities were resumed, had constantly fled before us, was now changing its tactics and turning right around to offer us battle. Benigsen, its general-in-chief, had taken this energetic resolve with strange suddenness, after the perusal of a bag of despatches captured on the person of one of the Prince of Neufchâtel's *aides-de-camp*. This officer had been sent over with orders for Marshal Bernadotte, but fell into Russian hands and by the documents he bore acquainted the enemy that our emperor at the time did not have his whole army within reach. General Benigsen concluded that he might offer battle with some chance of success, since his own entire force was concentrated in the vicinity.

From dawn of day the fire had continued along the whole line. Marshal Augereau had repeatedly done deeds of matchless valour with his army corps, which from twenty thousand men was reduced before

night to three thousand, but managed withal to keep in its possession the splendid vantage-ground it had won on the eve of the battle.

Exactly at three o'clock it became evident that the enemy was striving to cut our line of battle in two, and to that end a column of fifteen thousand Russian grenadiers had charged bayonets, and, without firing a shot, were rushing toward the centre of our position, despite of a terrible fire from thirty pieces of the Guard artillery placed in lottery upon the plateau of Eylau. This column advanced steadily at an even pace. The emperor, surrounded by his staff, said to Prince of Neufchâtel, while he kept his glass constantly directed toward the moving forest of bayonets:

"What daring! What extraordinary daring!"

"Extraordinary, indeed," replied Prince Berthier, "but Your Majesty does not perceive that this charge brings the enemy's column within a hundred paces of our bullets!"

"Murat," cried the emperor, "take all the cavalry you have at hand [there were about seventy squadrons, twenty of which belonged to the Imperial Guard under Marshal Bessières, who charged at their head] and crush out that column."

This order was executed on the moment and the brave phalanx of infantry was soon levelled to the earth like a wheat-field swept by a hurricane.

General D'Hautpoul, who commanded the *cuirassiers*, was killed, as was also General Dahlmann, commander of the *chasseurs* of the Guard. For a moment it was believed that General Lepic, who led the mounted grenadiers of the Guard, had been either killed or captured, for he did not reappear at the head of his troops when the corps was rallied. His ardour had carried him onward followed by a little troop of his men as far as the third line of the Russian infantry. One of the enemy's officers, who spoke French perfectly, rushed forward with a squadron of cavalry and having almost hemmed in the general and his brave grenadiers, shouted:

"Surrender. general! Your bravery has carried you too far; you are inside our lines!"

"Look at these faces," was the general's curt answer, "and see if they mean anything like surrender!" Then turning to his grenadiers he called out: "Follow me, men."

Facing right-about he again charged through the enemy's lines. More than half the brave fellows who followed him fell under the Russians' fire.

The emperor was delighted to see the general again, and riding up to him said:

"I thought you were taken prisoner, general, and it afflicted me deeply."

"You shall never hear other news than of my death, sire," replied the intrepid commander.

The Battle of Eylau cost the enemy seven thousand killed and fifteen thousand wounded, besides sixteen flags and twenty-four cannon captured; but what terrible efforts and losses that victory also occasioned to the French Army!

Next day, February 9th, our army bivouacked on the battlefield, which was still a mournful sight indeed. Our regiment had lost a great number of men, many killed and more wounded. The sergeant-major of the *Élite* company being disabled I had to call the muster-roll of its members. Out of one hundred men who rode in our ranks on the morning of the battle we had twenty-seven killed or wounded. Lieutenant Saint-Aubin was among the dead. He joined the company only a week and was killed by a pistol bullet fired at close range by a Russian officer.

On the 10th our brigade was incorporated with Prince Murat's cavalry. On the 15th, with the assistance of an infantry battalion, which had secured a wood to our right, we took possession of the village of

Trunkestein. From thence we could perceive the towers and steeples of Kœnigsberg, the second largest city in Prussia: we expected to occupy it and there recuperate our energies by the rest we so much needed. But the brigade was fated to endure a partial check, for on the very next day, toward three o'clock in the afternoon, our outposts, which were planted some distance beyond the village, were attacked not only in front but on either flank. The infantry battalion which carried the wood the day before had withdrawn and left it undefended, without giving us any notice. The enemy, now freed of opposition, was thus enabled to send some of its infantry along our right flank without being noticed, and soon began a fierce attack on several points at the same time. Our foremost squad galloped back to the main body, almost creating a panic: the brigade mounted as quickly as possible, but not before about fifty men had been killed or captured in the village. I was among the prisoners; my horse having been killed under me. I was wounded while stretched on the ground by five lance-thrusts. It was during this turmoil that Lieutenant Sourd of the 7th Chasseurs, now a general and baron of the Empire, one of the bravest soldiers in

the French Army, was wounded and made prisoner. From that event dates our old and cordial friendship.

My wounds, one of which was on the hip, caused me to limp in walking but did not prevent me from moving along slowly. After dragging me from under my horse the Cossacks went through my pockets and took possession of my belt within which they found a few stray *frederics*. The greater portion of my treasure I had hidden in the high collar of my coat, besides transforming several of the gold pieces into buttons. My friend Henri had advised me of this way to conceal from the enemy the bulk of my little fortune.

Since we left Holland our uniform had been altered. Instead of a dolman and pantaloons in the Hungarian style, we now wore coats with long tails and trousers having the inner side of the legs made of leather. There were plenty of buttons on this costume which could be substituted by golden *frederics*. I thus concealed about forty specimens of Prussian money Whenever I needed some change I would rip up a corner of my coat-collar or cut off one of my buttons.

Our captors led us to about half a league within their outposts. There we found the *hetman*, or commander of the Cossacks. As soon as he noticed my uniform he inquired whether I belonged to the corps against which the Cossacks and Russian dragoons had charged at Eylau. I answered that I did. He then congratulated me in pretty good French on belonging to such a valiant regiment. To these words of compliment he added some excellent French brandy and most palatable white bread. While I was finishing a meal such as I had not tasted for weeks he unfolded a map of France, and pointing out the departments composing the old provinces of Vendée and Bretagne, said:

"I suppose this is a part of France that does not supply Bonaparte with either men or money?"

"Allow me to say you are mistaken, general, in regard to war assessments; as far as conscripts are concerned, there are so many from that region that our army contains a multitude of soldiers who have entered the ranks as volunteers long before the age when conscription might claim them. For my own part I shall not have reached that age until next year."

The *hetman* ended our conversation with a sentence that characterizes both the rectitude of the Russian mind and its impregnable stubbornness:

"Yes, the Russians are learning from the French, but they will finish one of these days by knowing as much as their teachers."

At night we reached Kœnigsberg, where all the prisoners were lodged together in a large, unwarmed church, being allowed only a little straw for a bed and some "hard-tack" for food. We had there about fifty men from our brigade. The officers were treated somewhat better than the soldiers; they were assigned to decent lodgings but we failed to see them afterward.

Next day the surgeons made an inspection of the wounded prisoners, and I was sent to the hospital, where I remained only a few days, for our captors seemed to fear greatly the approach of the French Army. They soon sent us back as far as Wilna. During my stay in the hospital I had, as a neighbour, a young officer of the 14th Infantry; he had been wounded and taken on the 16th of February. He told me that just two weeks previously he was enjoying himself at the opera in Paris; on the 1st of February he graduated from the Military School of Fontainebleau, and left the same day by diligence to join his regiment in Poland. And the worst was yet to come, for he speedily died from his wounds in the Russian hospital.

Sleighs were driven to the gate of the hospital to carry us along the Wilna road. I remember that on the first day of our journey the forepart of our sleigh was loosened by some accident, and the horses trotted along leaving behind them the vehicle with four wounded men in it. It took a full hour to have the damage repaired, during which we suffered fearfully from the cold. I believe I suffered more then than at any other time in all my campaigns. I was only twenty years old, a prisoner of war, with five lance-wounds in my body, one of which on the left side was deep and painful. Add to this that my right foot was swollen, and I was also much troubled by a wound I had formerly received on the instep. I thanked Heaven when at last we reached Wilna a few days after we passed the river Niemen. Again they lodged us in a large church transformed into a hospital, it being situated not far from the city on the right bank of the Dwina. We had been there but a few days when I could walk with the help of crutches, and thus take advantage of the first beams of the early spring sun.

One day as I was thus promenading, gloomy enough in spirit, I noticed two ladies who were wrapped in enormous furs and driving along in a stylish sleigh, having on it a coachman and footman in livery. When this equipage reached the railing of the hospital grounds the horses were stopped and one of the ladies made me a most gracious sign to approach the spot. I walked over as promptly as I could—which was not very fast because of my wounded hip. I was greatly sur-

prised when I came close to the railing, which we were forbidden to pass, to hear a French voice inquire most kindly about my condition and that of my unfortunate comrades. The ladies questioned me as to my age, my rank in the army, and the part of France I came from.

The lively interest with which we inspired these amiable visitors did not confine itself to asking questions, for as soon as Madame Drémon—this was the lady's name—heard that there were three hundred in the hospital she asked me whether there were any officers among us. On my replying in the negative she begged me to take charge of a sum of one thousand paper *rubles*, equal to about one thousand *francs*, and handed them to me in a small pocketbook, to be divided among

my dear compatriots. I accepted this mission with much gratitude.
Having returned to the hospital, I invited one of my regimental comrades to come to my assistance. Each man received three *rubles*, and
adding the sixteen surplus *rubles*—for we were at the time only two
hundred and eighty—to the three which were their proper share, I divided the remainder between two prisoners more seriously wounded
than the rest, and who were therefore in greater need of money.

On the Sunday following our comfortress did not fail to come
again to see us, as she had promised to do. She rode in the same equipage. After the usual greetings I gave her a statement of the use I
had made of her money, asking her as a special favour to allow me to

retain the pocketbook. She next inquired if it would give me pleasure to accept her hospitality, and she sent into the hospital by her footman a large bundle of hosiery, shirts and shoes that were provided for us by the French residents of Wilna. Then she left me, promising to speak in my behalf to the governor.

Three days later Madame Drémon redeemed her promise by calling to take me to be introduced to the governor. She was provided with the necessary permit, but informed me how she had been obliged to state that I was a relative of hers, adding with a smile: "Although you come from Paris and I from Nancy, we might be cousins, you know, just the same!"

I was lavish in my expressions of gratitude. We soon arrived on the principal square of the city and in front of a beautiful store which Madame Drémon pointed out to me, saying:

"That is my home, but we must first go to General Korsakoff's office."

A short distance beyond the sleigh was stopped before a large door, guarded on both sides by sentries. This was the governor's dwelling. A footman led us to the second floor, where we found General Korsakoff seated by a huge fire. He arose when he recognized Madame Drémon, and inquiring after her health with much politeness, offered her a seat. I had to stand leaning against a piece of furniture, using my crutches as a prop. Everything was arranged as the lady desired and the general accorded the favour asked for me.

Madame Drémon's store was also the habitation of several young ladies employed by her who were, I was told, either Polish or German. It was a very imposing establishment devoted to the sale of millinery, dry-goods, chinaware, glassware, and so forth—in fact an extensive commission house for all Parisian merchandise. A clerk, who spoke German, Russian and French, acted as superintendent of the sales department.

Madame Drémon had the kindness to cause a room to be prepared for me on the lower floor and there I sojourned for ten weeks, an object of the most refined attentions. At length came the time for leaving, but as we exchanged goodbye, my "fair cousin," who had attended to all the preparations for my journey, placed a small package in my hand, saying;

"Here are two books, dear cousin, which I ask you not to show to anyone before you have read them yourself! You will find them both instructive and amusing."

"You shall be obeyed, as you ever should be, angel of kindness"—
and with a heavy heart I bade *adieu* to Madame Drémon, whom I was
never to see again.

The detachment set out on the road to Kovno. At the first stopping
place we were lodged four or five together in the homes of the peas-
antry, who for our excellent money supplied us only with milk and
potatoes. One may imagine that it was not long before I opened the

two books Madame Drémon had given me: they were *Caesar's Commentaries* in French and Latin. Between each of the first ten pages of the first volume I found a banknote of one hundred *rubles*, amounting in all to one thousand. Such a delicate way of providing for my wants during the rest of my captivity made my regard still deeper for this most amiable lady.

Between Wilna and Kovno we were met by the Emperor Alexander, who was on his way to his army. He passed our detachment in review. I paraded at its head, being the only non-commissioned officer present. He spoke to us very graciously, and asked us whether we had any complaint to make as to the treatment we were receiving.

As we had really no cause for complaint, none was formulated. The emperor seemed satisfied and gave the detachment a sum of money amounting to one *ducat* for each man. I tendered him thanks in the name of my unfortunate companions, and he went on his way.

Two hours' journey from the city of Kovno, on the same day, we met two regiments of Baskirs on their way to join the army. Their principal weapon was the bow and arrows, and that inspired our soldiers to nickname them the Cupids of the Russian army. I hardly think that such troops could fight on even terms with ours. A *chasseur* from our regiment called Vandiselberg, rather too generously favoured in the matter of nose, was the only one I ever knew that was hit by a Baskir's arrow.

"If you had not such a long and clumsy nose," his comrades would say, "that Cupid's arrow would have passed by without leaving a mark."

At Kovno, after an extremely modest meal, we noticed as we were walking about a large building, which we were informed was a convent. I proposed to the two *chasseurs* who were with me to enter it and make a call. They consented and we walked up the vestibule into the reception room, where we were courteously received. All the nuns (it was a sisters' convent) came to the lattice partition. Among them was one young lady of good family who spoke French perfectly. She was a boarder in the convent, but had not taken the vows; her worldly attire was sufficient evidence of the fact.

I ventured to ask her if it was really her determination to withdraw from the world, as she seemed to be endowed with all the qualities that would make her a brilliant social success. She answered me that she had but one month longer to stay within the convent walls, where she had been living for some time in virtue of a custom very general among the women of the Polish nobility.

Thanks to this charming interpreter we had no trouble in making ourselves understood by the sisters, who seemed to feel regret when informed that we had already dined. But as we were to spend a few days in Kovno, we promised to return on the morrow.

Next day at noon there were five of us seated in the refectory. Our hostesses served us some excellent soup, boiled beef and bacon, also sauerkraut and potatoes, and plenty of beer and cognac. We heartily thanked the good sisters, who were very piously impressed when one of our number, before the unfolding of napkins, arose and recited in a clear sonorous voice, and in Latin, the whole formula of the blessing before meat.

The following day we continued our route toward Minsk and Smolensk, and after sojourning a week in the latter city, proceeded in the direction of Wolmir and Kalouga. Wladimir was the terminus of our journey, for the news of the peace had just readied that city. We straightway retraced our steps over the same highway as far as Smolensk, then through Warsaw, when we entered on the Pomeranian road to join our command. On the 13th of October we reached Stolp, where the staff of our regiment was in cantonments; we had been absent over eight mouths. When we presented ourselves at Colonel Castex' lodgings, he was just leaving the breakfast table.

"Hello!" he cried, "here are my children back again. How much you must have suffered, my gallant boys!"

I answered for all: "Past sufferings are forgotten in the joy of beholding our dear regiment, with Colonel Castex still at its head."

"Indeed!" exclaimed the colonel, in his Gascon accent, smiling good-humouredly. "Then I thank you all for the affection you have ever borne me."

He soon dismissed us, at the same time directing that we should return to our old companies, and that I should resume my rank as quartermaster of the Élite company, as that post had not been filled. I leave the reader to fancy how delighted I was to re-enter upon my old duties.

But my greatest happiness was to again meet my friend Henri. He had received during the campaign the cross of the Legion of Honour and when I congratulated him on it, answered me smilingly:

"I owe it entirely to my mare Schipska."

"Are you jesting?" I inquired. "Please tell me all about it."

"You are certainly not in luck, my poor Parquin, for on the day that followed your capture our regiment started back toward its previous quarters, and the squadrons were recruited both in men and horses. After three months spent in that comfortable locality, the army again advanced, full of fight. We met the enemy almost daily, and in every single encounter our regiment kept up its gallant reputation.

At the bloody fight of Guttstadt General Lasalle's division, to which
our regiment belonged, was constantly under the artillery fire of the
enemy; we had been posted so as to hide a flank march undertaken by
an infantry division, which reached the wood and turned the enemy
on the left. During the entire day our regiment had been pestered by
a crowd of Cossacks, whom our *chasseurs* charged frequently but could
never reach, for in accordance with their usual tactics the Cossacks
would gallop back under cover of the Russian artillery, which occasioned us heavy losses by suddenly unmasking its batteries.

"The colonel, who had become greatly worried by these repeated
manoeuvres, which left us in a bad predicament, took advantage of the
fact that our infantry was for a moment in possession of a clump of
woods on the right, to give Captain Bertin the order to sweep round
the timber with his squadron, so as to be able to charge the enemy
as soon as he should hear the musketry fire, and then dash across the
plateau at full speed toward the main body of the regiment. Captain
Bertin had not been gone five minutes when the colonel galloped
over to Lieutenant Capitan, and gave him the following order:

"Lieutenant, you will set out on the trot with your squad [of which I was one] and place yourself ten feet in front of the outskirts of the woods [and he showed him a spot three or four hundred feet away]. Let your front rank then make ready with carbines; as soon as the enemy see you they will charge in a complete body but not until they are about six feet from you, must you give the order to fire. They will quickly charge again and again, and your men will probably be sabred and trampled under the hoofs of their heavy squadrons; but you are not to retreat. Remember, sir, I shall have my eye upon you.'"

"Both these orders were carried out with the same precision with which they had been given, for not until the moment our troops were charged by the enemy and were actually at close quarters, did we fire off our carbines.

"Just then the squadron under the command of Captain Bertin rushed in upon the plateau and charged the Cossacks, who, being thus surprised in the rear by the captain's force, and attacked in front by ours, which had now taken the offensive, and thus sabred and cut down on both sides at the same time, had to admit themselves van-

quished, and besides strewing the ground with their dead and wounded furnished us with a considerable number of prisoners.

"Indeed, I feel, my dear Parquin, that the fight at Guttstadt has
avenged us fully for the unlucky affair of February 15th at Trunkestein,
when you and so many of our friends were wounded and captured."

"Now tell me," I said to Henri, "what was the brave deed that
earned you the cross? You have modestly credited your horse with being the cause of your getting it and I should very much like to know
how such a miracle came about."

"It is the simple truth," retorted Henri, "just listen and judge for
yourself."

And he related to me the following facts:

"During the sanguinary Battle of Heilsberg, on the 11th of June, I
had been appointed one of the orderlies of Prince Murat. You know
him—he is the general-in-chief of all our cavalry—is always dressed
up like a drum-major—and is as fond of meeting the enemy at close
quarters as any of his hussars.

"Well, about two o'clock on that eventful afternoon Prince Murat moved toward the point where the emperor then was, that is, in the centre of a division of grenadiers, under command of General Oudinot. The emperor and this general had dismounted upon an elevated plateau, from which His Majesty was inspecting the enemy's position through his field-glass.

"As soon as he arrived Prince Murat dismounted and giving his horse into my charge, advanced to salute the emperor: he then shook hands with General Oudinot and began a conversation with him. Suddenly a cloud of dust arose directly in front of us—the emperor looked at it through his glass and asked Prince Murat:

"'What is the meaning of that, sir?'

"'It is nothing, sire.'

"'What do you mean by nothing? Please go look at it more closely.'"

As he uttered these words, the emperor made a lively slash with his whip across the flank of Prince Murat's horse, which the latter had just remounted. General Oudinot had meanwhile urged upon the emperor to retire within one of the grenadier squares, saying to him, with the usual sarcasm of an infantry general when speaking of horsemen:

"'It is nothing, sire. It is only your cavalry making a charge rearward'

"The prince, his staff, and myself had started forward on a gallop.

"'Follow me with your regiment,' ordered the prince, as he passed close to Colonel Dery, commander of the 5th Hussars, 'and let us charge this rabble.'

"In another minute we were at close quarters with the enemy and were beginning to use our sabres to excellent purpose, when a cannonball struck down the prince's charger. I dismounted in a jiffy and while clinging to my horse's bridle helped the prince to get out from beneath his own. He was obliged to leave his left boot in the stirrup.

"'It is nothing—nothing,' said the prince. 'Let me have a horse.'

"I at once offered mine, which was accepted, and the prince mounted with one foot having a boot on and the other stripped. Indeed, it was not to fly out of danger that the prince had asked for my horse; on the contrary, it was to rush into the fray, shouting at the top of his voice, 'Forward! Forward! Long live the Emperor!' and within a quarter of an hour three or four thousand Cossacks who had taken possession of the plateau were swept away like chaff.

" I took good care to carry the prince's saddle back to his headquarters, and I assure you it was a heavy load, for there was more gold in it than steel. The same evening Prince Murat had my horse returned to me and inquired for the number of my regiment and my name. I received the cross of the Legion of Honour after the close of the campaign. So you see, my dear Parquin, that I really am indebted to Schipska for the honour bestowed upon me. Of course I had slashed and cut down many a Cossack while riding beside the prince; but I hardly think he noticed what I was then doing."

"You are as brave as you are modest, my dear Henri, and well worthy to bear the cross of the Legion, especially because of an act which others have already told me of—I mean the rescue from captivity, on February 15th, of Lieutenant Dupont, who had been wounded by a lance-thrust in the eye."

"Oh, yes," replied Henri, "I forgot to tell you about that: but indeed I was delighted to be of service to an officer who was so beloved by our regiment, and who is now, I learn, an iron manufacturer near Dinant, in Belgium Before he left the regiment he forced me to accept a gift of six hundred *francs*; nor did I dare to decline it, as I knew that my refusal would pain him very much."

"By the way," I asked Henri, "was our regiment at the famous Battle of Friedland?"

"I should think so! Is there ever any such picnic in which the regiment bearing the proud number '20' does not take a part? We were not actively engaged there, it is true, but we had a number of men and horses killed. In the evening, quite late, we were sent out to pursue the enemy. Next morning, which was the 15th, we came up with the rearguard, and our regiment was ungallant enough to slash and cut down the Cupids of the Russian Army, the Baskirs. Their arrows did not do us much damage, although some people say they are poisoned. Only one *chasseur* was wounded, and he did not die. Those Prussian hussars who sport the death's heads on their shakos, and are none the braver on that account, tried to avenge the Baskirs' unfortunate fate, but they could not even break our ranks, although much more numerous than we, and our regiment soon put them to full flight and drove them hotly up the road to Kœnigsberg. Marshal Soult's corps entered that city on the 14th of June, and we were supplied with excellent lodgings on Nogat Island, in old Prussia, where all the cavalry of Prince Murat had rendezvoused. General Lasalle, who commanded our division, had his headquarters at Elbing. This commander was as fond of good eating as he was of fighting, and contrived a funny way of inviting to dinner the officers of his division who rode toward their cantonments through Elbing.

"The general's butler, an hour before dinner time, would tie up against the balcony of his house a napkin attached to a stick. As long as twenty seats—reserved at the general's table for the stray guests who might drop in—were not occupied, the napkin fluttered to the wind, and the officers of the division who saw the token were free to step upstairs and call upon their general, being sure of an invitation to dinner. But if the napkin had been withdrawn, it was useless to try potluck: the table was filled.

"This same General Lasalle made a very witty answer to one of the
emperor's questions, when the latter, on July 5th, held a review of the
whole cavalry corps.

"During this parade, His Majesty had been very lavish in his distribution of promotions and decorations. The general, however, did not
seem satisfied. "'What is the matter? the emperor asked him. 'Are you
not pleased, general?'

"'I am deeply grateful for Your Majesty's kindness, sire; but if I must tell the truth, I am not yet satisfied. I did hope that Your Majesty would deign to think of me as commandant of the first regiment in the world: in a word, I did hope to be called to the command of your Guides to succeed General Dahlmann.'

"The emperor answered: 'When General Lasalle has ceased swearing and smoking, not only shall I appoint him to a regiment of my cavalry of the Guard, but I shall also make him one of my chamberlains.'

"General Lasalle bowed deeply, and said to His Majesty: 'Sire, since it appears that I have all the necessary qualities for a seaman, I humbly beg Your Majesty to give me command of a frigate.'

"'No, no, that would never do,' replied the emperor smiling, 'I appoint you commander of the twenty regiments of cavalry in the absence of Prince Murat.'

"During the same review, the emperor showered honours upon our regiment. Colonel Castex and our two majors were made officers of the Legion of Honour; the captain of our company was promoted to be major. When the latter officer was presented to the emperor,

His Majesty asked him how many years he had been a captain, and he answered: 'Fifteen years, sire.'

"'This officer must surely have been forgotten,' said the emperor, and he immediately gave him his promotion."

"When Captain Pequinot came forward in his turn, the emperor asked him also how long he had been a captain. Pequinot answered: 'For fourteen years, sire.'

"The emperor looked surprised, and at once promoted him major and made him a captain in the horse grenadiers of the Guard; Captain Kirmann, with thirteen years' service as captain, was promoted to be major and a captain in the Guard *chasseurs*. Finally, when Captain Lion presented himself and responded that he had been captain seven years, the emperor said curtly; 'Too young an officer.' But the colonel retorted right away: 'Allow me, sire, to call Your Majesty's attention to the fact that Captain Lion only seems so young on account of his being introduced immediately after a number of officers who have held their rank for such a long time.'

101

"The emperor, who had already walked on, paused a moment on hearing this remark, and noticing a deep scar across the face of Captain Lion, asked him: 'Where did you receive that sabre-slash that adorns your face?'

"'At Ulm, sire.'

"On the spot the captain was promoted major, and sent to the 14th Chasseurs.

"The amusing point was that his answer, although literally true, was

in effect a brazen falsehood. Of course the emperor understood from Captain Lion's words that his wound had been received in the Battle of Ulm, when in fact it was incurred in a duel which he fought while in bivouac at that place. The emperor, who abhorred and discouraged duels, would never have promoted Captain Lion had he known the truth.

'That is all the news, my dear Parquin, that I can give you of any interest, for after these events we remained throughout the winter in our cantonments on the island of Nogat.'

Such was the narrative of Henri which I have here accurately reproduced.

Our regiment left Silesia during the first days of April, 1808, and marched toward the shores of the Baltic, where we found new quarters in the neighbourhood of Dantzic. The regimental staff and the Élite company, to which I belonged, had their cantonments in a little city called Lauenbourg, where we sojourned for six months.

This place is almost fourteen leagues from Dantzic. the quartermasters had to go to the larger city every four days to procure white bread for our soup and the soldiers' ration bread. At the close of December, 1808, I was returning from this distribution, and as usual, the *chasseurs* detailed to accompany us were, like myself, wrapped up in their cloaks and stretched upon the straw in the wagons. When night came on, as we were about two leagues distant from Lauenbourg, the leading wagon stopped and wild shrieks of terror caused us all to jump down and out of the vehicles. We rushed at once, sabres drawn, over the now-covered road toward the head of the convoy, whence the shrieks were heard. The alarm had been occasioned by a pack of wolves, the regular denizens of the forest we had just been crossing, and which had thrown themselves with desperate voracity on the horses and the foremost wagons containing the bread. The peasants who were driving the wagons sought safety beneath them. The *chas-*

seurs and myself, after killing and wounding a number of the wolves, were at length fain to admit that it was impossible to vanquish the whole pack, so we had to make our escape as best we could by abandoning all the wagons except two, which had not yet been attacked, and leaving to the infuriated animals the horses and supplies they had already virtually captured.

CHAPTER 2

Austria
1809

On the 1st day of January, 1809, we quitted for good and all the Prussian territory, but before starting off we were informed by an order of the emperor that out of the war contributions exacted from that monarchy he had forestalled a sum of one hundred million *francs* to be distributed among the troops. Every soldier of the army, be he non-commissioned officer or private, was to receive fifteen *francs* if he had been in arms at the Battle of Jena; if he had been present also at Eylau he was entitled to thirty *francs*; and if his campaign included the Battle of Friedland he was to receive forty-five *francs*. Moreover, every soldier who had been wounded was entitled to the maximum amount. I was of course included in this last category and was paid the sum of forty-five *francs*.

When we reached the cantonments prepared for us, near Frankfort-on-the-Main, we found that the regimental staff and the Élite company were to be quartered in the beautiful village of Bockenheim, where most of the houses are occupied by Jews. It was during our sojourn there that my friend Henri one day said to me:

"Eh, Parquin, old fellow, don't you suppose 'The Little Corporal' will set his *chapeau* crosswise again? Don't you think he'll soon get vicious again? Don't you fancy we'll have another campaign? Aren't you and I just itching for it?"—and he touched his burly shoulder on the spot where a lieutenant's epaulet would go. "And you," he added "here, and here?" pointing this time both at my shoulder and at my breast, where as yet there was no cross of the Legion of Honour.

Alas, the brave fellow had no presentiment that the campaign he so ardently desired would yield him a glorious death upon the field of battle!

We remained in that cantonment until the 1st of March and enjoyed ourselves greatly by being so near to the city of Frankfort. Once I went as far as Hanan, the headquarters of General Oudinot, to whom I had an introduction. The general received me very kindly and when I was coming away said that he would shortly have some news for me. A week later Colonel Castex sent for me and asked whether I cared to be appointed sergeant in the fifth company, but as I declined to leave the Élite company even for sake of promotion the matter was dropped. One month later. Sergeant Jouglas having been appointed to some other post, I was promoted to be sergeant in the Élite company itself.

I was far from expecting the strange incident that befell me when I left the village of Bockenheim. For two months and a half I had been billeted at the house of a rich Jew, the rabbi of the neighbouring synagogue. He was a widower and had an only daughter, named Sarah, a tall, dark-featured and beautifully-formed young lady. She was scarcely twenty years old, and was in charge of a school for the little girls of the commune. I had lived on excellent terms with my hosts and was always very courteous and obliging toward Mlle. Sarah, but beyond that our intercourse had never extended. On the day of departure I left my lodgings at about five in the morning, without feeling any regrets myself and with no idea that I was leaving any behind me. We had hardly set out on the road to Frankfort when, in rummaging my sabretache, I discovered that I had forgotten a small memorandum book in which I used to jot down notes concerning the regiment. The adjutant gave me permission to return for it and I rode back to my old lodgings. I found the door wide open, as my orderly had forgotten to close it when he quitted the house after me. I bounded up the stairs without knocking and speedily reached my room, which was on the second floor facing the street. How astonished was I to find therein the beautiful Sarah gazing at my empty chair and visibly in tears. She was attired in her breakfast gown, and her long silky hair fell scattered over her shoulders. At hurried intervals she caressed with kisses my poor little memorandum book. Though amazed at the unexpected sight I soon recovered composure enough to advance toward the young lady and to address her in my tenderest voice: "You here, Sarah?"

"Yes," she said, " I am here and weeping about you, you insensible man!" And her tears began to flow more abundantly than before.

Much moved by this explosion of feeling, which was evidently sincere, I took the impressionable Sarah's hand and by kind and cheering words, with more vows of love and fidelity than I dare to say, soon managed to console her.

Happy moments are ever the most fleeting. The neighing of my steed, which the orderly held by the bridle in front of the house, recalled me to the urgency of military duties and I was compelled to take leave of the tender Sarah, who returned my memorandum book, only begging me to tear out and give her the page on which my name was inscribed. Immediately I wrote down her own name beside mine, adding also the date as being the happiest day in my life. At least, I assured her so, and I wrapped up in the leaf of paper a ring made out of my hair—of which I had more than one. The gift had a magical effect.

"How happy you make me, Charles," she said to me, "by giving me this ring. But we must now part, for if my father should find that I had held the least converse with you he would look upon it as a serious indiscretion."

I tore myself from the presence of the tender Jewess and was still rather agitated by my transient flirtation as I galloped quickly away.

Thirty years later, when leaving Switzerland, I passed through Frankfort, where I stayed for a couple of days at the house of my friend, M. de Saint-Georges, a partner in the banking house of Bethman & Co. After having dined together in the society of his family we two old comrades adjourned to his picture gallery to smoke some excellent Spanish cigarettes. I told him of my ancient love affair with the handsome Jewess at Bockenheim, and I added: "This morning, although the weather was rather chilly for a ride, I thought I would mount horse and pay a visit to Bockenheim to learn what had become of Sarah. I had ridden about half the distance when I bethought myself that if she were married she must be now a matron of at least fifty years, surrounded by children and perhaps grandchildren. So I said to myself, 'I shall meet but the wreck of what was once the young and graceful Sarah: and instead of the bright sketch I have so long carried in memory I shall see only a faded, antique picture that would crush my cherished illusions. No, I shall not do that: and turning my horse's head. I rode back to Frankfort.'"

M. de Saint-Georges, who had heard me attentively, made the remark: "Colonel, a German would have gone on, not afraid to meet the woman who was once his Sarah, even after thirty years of separation."

"Well, well," I answered "we Frenchmen are entirely different; we are much more emotional and therefore more sentimental."

When we crossed Bavaria, during March, 1809, our regiment stopped for a few weeks at Baireuth and in the neighbouring villages. Being still quartermaster of the Élite I was lodged with the regimental staff in the city itself. The captain of the company having ordered an inspection for the first Sunday after our arrival I went around through the city to obtain the different articles required by my orderly to put uniforms and weapons in condition. While doing so I entered the store of a grocer and haberdasher, situated on the square opposite my quarters. I was agreeably surprised to find that the owner of this establishment was a remarkable bright and good looking young lady. Being much more impressed by her attractions than with the object of my call, I was some moments in the place before remembering for what I had come, and it was only when she addressed me a second time that I realized I had any other purpose than gazing at a pretty woman's face.

The next day, quite early, I entered the store to make some further purchases. A man who happened to be present and who seemed to be about double the age of the lady, was good enough to reveal to me his wife's Christian name, for he addressed her in German—a language which I understood pretty well at the time—saying: "Ludzig, pass me the box of gentlemen's gloves."

This call for gloves had been inspired by the demand of a friend of mine who had accompanied me into the store. It was thus that on my second visit I was informed of the lady's given name, and being already much fascinated by her I was not long in making use of it. On the third day, having watched from my window the time when the tradesman left, I immediately entered the store again, under pretence of buying a few knick-knacks. There were several customers in at the time, and all I could do to further my wooing was to show the lady as I saluted her that I held a letter in my hand. Having left the store I thought my pretensions were abortive and endeavoured to console myself for the failure. While entering the *porte-cochère* of the house in which I lived, however, I felt myself pulled by the coat-tail. It was done by one of the shop-girls. She did not even give me time to ask what she wished, but said to me at once: "Where is the letter?"

"Here it is," I answered, for I still held it in the palm of my hand.

This *billet-doux* was worded as follows—a non-commissioned officer of my regiment, named Gasner, having been kind enough to translate it into German for me:

"Charming Ludzig:—I am yearning for the happiness of meet-

ing you alone and telling you how deeply I have been impressed by your beauty. Do find some means of granting me this privilege, and you will make me the happiest of men. In the meantime I caress your dainty hand. Charles P."

A quarter of an hour later the messenger returned with an answer, to my notion as short and significant as the request.

"Tomorrow, Saturday, at seven o'clock in the evening, my husband is going to an amateur concert in which he takes a part. I shall then be free until nine o'clock. Come to the back alley at a quarter past seven. The store will be closed, but you will be conducted to my presence."

There is no need to say that I was punctual at the rendezvous. I had barely entered a very dark alley when somebody seized my hand. It was the shop-girl, who led me along the alley, across a small yard filled with casks and boxes and thence into a narrow passage. There my guide opened a door to the left, and ushering me into a room that was lighted only by a fire left me, having first whispered the word; "Silence!"

A minute later the door was opened again and the fluttering of a silk dress betokened the arrival of the lady of the house.

"Ludzig, is it you?"

"*Ya*," she answered, "it is I, Charles."

And like a true German she greeted me very cordially. But that was all—for it was with pity rather than favour that she then heard my ardent suit and reproved me for its unseemliness. Evidently she considered me as a mere giddy boy.

The lady then excused herself for not offering me luncheon, as she would have to light the lamps or candles, and that would make my visit the pretext of scandal. All she could do was to bring in some excellent Spanish wine with biscuits, which she hospitably presented to me and which I found so pleasant and appetizing as to tempt me to other visits on the succeeding Saturdays, in spite of the wound that my self-conceit had encountered. The regiment left Baireuth at the end of a month. I had to say goodbye to the kindly shop-woman, from whose husband I had daily purchased everything the company needed, so that we had grown to be great friends and he insisted that I accept the stirrup-cup from his own hand. Just as I left the amiable Ludzig of course said goodbye to me, but I looked in vain for demonstrations of regret, though on the previous day she had intimated to me cordially that I was as dear to her as an only son.

Our regiment continued its way toward Augsburg and we took

quarters in the vicinity of that city. On the 10th of April, 1809, Prince Charles addressed Marshal Davoust the following letter which was put on the order of the day:

"To the General-in-chief of the French Army in Bavaria:

"In accordance with a declaration from the Emperor of Austria, addressed to the Emperor Napoleon, I notify the general-in-chief of the French Army that my orders are to march forward with the troops under my command, and to treat as enemies all forces that may attempt to impede our advance.

"Given at my headquarters, April 9th, 1809."

Marshal Davoust had this letter published to his troops, announcing at same time that he would concentrate the army at once, so as to attack the enemy that had dared, believing itself the stronger, to violate the territory of our allies.

The emperor, who had been notified on the 12th, in Paris, of the forward march of the Austrians, arrived on the 17th at Donawerth in Bavaria, whence he addressed to the army the following proclamation:

"Soldiers!

"The territory of the Rhenish Confederation has been violated. The Austrian general expects us to flee at the sight of his guns. With lightning rapidity I have joined the army. Soldiers! I was among you when the Austrian sovereign came over to my bivouac in Moravia, and you heard him implore my clemency and pledge me eternal friendship. Three times his conquerors, the Emperor owes everything to our generosity; three times he has perjured himself. Our past successes are a sure guarantee of triumphs to come. Let us march forward, therefore, so that the enemy, on seeing us, may recognize his masters!"

This proclamation was received with enthusiasm by the whole army.

At that time we served as vanguard to the grenadiers assembled under General Oudinot's command, General Colbert being at the head of our brigade, which was composed of the 7th and 20th Chasseurs and the 9th Hussars. It had been nicknamed the "Infernal Brigade."

From the 10th to the 19th our army corps manoeuvred between Munich and Augsburg, but on the latter date we took part in some lively fighting when four thousand Austrians were dispersed or made prisoners at the Battle of Pfaffenhoffen, The 7th Chasseurs distinguished themselves by a brilliant charge and captured most of the prisoners. Our brigade followed the enemy and we engaged them several times before we reached Ratisbon, on the morning of the 23rd—the day on which the emperor, venturing too near the batteries of the fortress, was wounded in the heel. This news spread through the army like wildfire and produced an immense sensation. The staff officers of the emperor were despatched from his headquarters in all directions to reassure the army concerning the gravity of His Majesty's wound, General Lauriston, one of the emperor's *aides-de-camp*, whose son had recently joined our regiment as lieutenant, himself came to assure us that the emperor had been but slightly hurt.

On the following day Marshal Davoust gained the Battle of Eckmuhl, the name of which was bestowed on him with a princely dignity. The King of Bavaria had just returned to his capital, which had suffered from the treacherous invasion of the Austrians. The latter were now in full retreat at all points, and accordingly, the emperor before leaving Ratisbon took occasion to thank the army in these words:

"Soldiers! You have fulfilled my expectation. Your bravery has supplied all deficiency of numbers. In a few days you have won the three battles of Thann, Abensberg and Eckmuhl, as well as the fights of Landshut and Ratisbon. The enemy, deceived by statesmen who disregard their promises, seemed to have forgotten all about you; but

you appeared and showed yourselves more terrible than ever. Only a
few weeks ago they crossed the river Inn and invaded the territory
of our allies. Only a few weeks ago they boasted that they would
carry the war even into our own fatherland. Today, vanquished and
terror-stricken, they flee before us in disorder! Already my vanguard
has passed the Inn within a month from now we shall be in Vienna."

It was General Colbert's brigade that had crossed the Inn. On April 30th General Oudinot requested the emperor to appoint six non commissioned officers from each regiment of the vanguard, as candidates in waiting, to take the place of officers who might drop out of the ranks during the approaching campaign.

On the 6th of May at ten o'clock in the morning our regiment, which on that day held the head of the Colbert brigade, came in contact with the enemy's rearguard in the village of Amstetten; for the Austrians were retreating toward Saint-Pölten in the direction of Vienna. A pretty lively skirmish took place on that occasion, when Lieutenant Lacour was wounded in the arm, and a few of our *chasseurs* lost their horses, shot down by the enemy's infantry, who occupied a wood on the left of the road. At eleven o'clock a flag of truce was sent to General Colbert by the Austrians. The commander of the enemy's rearguard begged for one hour's suspension of hostilities, which was granted him.

Since dawn of day the regiment had been in the saddle and both men and horses were in dire need of a rest. Colonel Castex immediately gave the order to unbridle the chargers and give them an hour at their oats, a supply of which every *chasseur* carried along with him, A wide rivulet ran close to the spot where we had come to a halt, and was of great use to us in watering our horses. Thus we employed this hour of respite to best advantage, and the *chasseurs* ate a crust of bread flavoured with garlic and drank a gulp or two of brandy,—a very modest breakfast enjoyed all the more keenly from a conviction that by noon we should be hotly engaged with the enemy.

Five minutes before the hour expired the trumpets again sounded "To horse," and the colonel gave orders for cloaks to be rolled tight and carried crosswise: a preliminary which all knew well to mean that we were on the point of charging. We had been formed in battle array; volunteers were called out to act as skirmishers; and we were about starting, when Colonel Castex, riding in front of the Élite company, called out to me:

"Sergeant Parquin, I have your brevet as second-lieutenant in my sabretache."

He had just received an answer to his request for six candidate-officers among those the emperor had granted to General Oudinot, and I was among the favoured ones.

"Long live the Emperor!" I shouted.

And addressing myself to the *chasseurs* of my squad, who were all congratulating me, I cried:

"*Chasseurs!* Now that I am promoted officer, I am entitled to have two chargers; if I do not manage to capture them myself from the Uhlans, I count upon you to supply me with mounts."

"Don't worry, lieutenant," replied my brave *chasseurs*, "we shall take care to fill your stable properly."

120

They kept their word, for the men of my company captured twenty-two Uhlans or hussars, and hunted for me everywhere to give me the first choice of horses. Unfortunately I had been carried over to the ambulance, having been wounded—and besides I had myself captured two excellent steeds. But let us return to the regiment just before it began the charge and proceed in order.

We had broken regimental formation and were now in squads, having advanced about a thousand feet upon Saint-Pölten, when we perceived the enemy in a double line of battle across the plateau. The first line was formed by six squadrons of lancers, the second by as many squadrons of hussars. We discovered an hour later that these lancers were almost all recruits from Austrian-Poland. Poles they were indeed so far as concerned their gallantry and the clever way in which they handled their lances. And yet they succumbed in the hand-to-hand fight with our regiment and the 7th Chasseurs, even though they were assisted by the Barko Hussars, famed throughout the Austrian Empire for their extreme bravery.

Both Uhlans and hussars were either sabred or put to flight. We pursued them for over two hours, and cut down and captured about three hundred men. General Oudinot, who was thoroughly posted on the merits of campaign fighting, frankly declared that he found the results achieved by his vanguard preferable to the capture of ten thousand militiamen.

I must here narrate a curious episode of which one of our comrades was the hero. During the hour of bivouac, and while our regiment was watering the horses, one of these animals, running wild, dashed close to the colonel, who was bivouacking in the centre of the regiment, and almost crippled him by a rearward kick. The colonel, noticing from the horse's colour that he must belong to the second squadron, ordered Second-Lieutenant Grignon, whose command it was, to have the horse caught and brought back to the ranks. I don't remember through what accident the colonel's order was unfulfilled, but the horse, revelling in his liberty, made a second wild gallop across the bivouac. Annoyed to see his orders so loosely attended to the colonel placed Lieutenant Grignon under arrest. To order an officer in arrest was to deprive him of his sabre. Just then the trumpeter again sounded "To horse," and our skirmishers had already joined issue with the enemy. The young officer, terribly upset and grieved, approached the colonel and begged to have his sword, of which the adjutant had taken possession. He pleaded that he had just exchanged into this regiment and that it was the first time his troop would have a chance to see him face the enemy. Colonel Castex refused and thus answered his appeal:

"I have resolved to punish you, sir, and this is why your sabre is taken away from you for the day."

"So it was not to prevent me from fighting the enemy?" demanded Lieutenant Grignon.

Then without waiting for reply he set spurs to his horse, and, pistol in hand, dashed into the strife, where he speedily shot down one of the Mervold Lancers; he next seized the dead man's lance and thus equipped went on charging the enemy. The same evening the colonel, who was apprised of the gallant style in which the young lieutenant had borne himself, complimented him publicly and had his sabre returned to him by the adjutant.

I am sorry to say that this valiant officer, for whom I had contracted a most cordial friendship, died during the disastrous Russian campaign, being at that time a captain in the regiment.

While speaking of the fight of May 6th, 1809, which proved so glorious for the 20th Chasseurs, I must not omit the credit to which the 7th is entitled. These two regiments, attached for so long a time to the same brigade, always enjoyed the most pleasant intercourse and were delighted to help each other in every way on the battlefield. On the occasion when the Uhlans were joined by the Barko Hussars this corps paused in its retreat and rallied back to the fight. At that moment, so critical for the 20th, which was overborne on all sides by the enemy and had only a narrow bridge as a path of retreat, Colonel Castex and his officers flung themselves into the gap, charging repeatedly, and held the enemy at bay, long enough to give the 7th an opening to the rescue and time to the squadrons of the 20th to repair their shattered formation.

In this *mêlée*, Colonel Castex shouted a few words, which still ring in my ears: "Rally around me, *chasseurs*, or you will lose the fruits of the most splendid battle charge ever made!"

At this very moment a Barko Hussar, in scant courtesy, broke in on the colonel with a sabre-stroke of such vigour as to cleave his cartridge-box in two. Our commander feeling himself hit, swung his horse around to face the trouble, shouting as he did so:

"What is this youngster up to?"

"This youngster" had already ceased to exist, for just as he was dealing another blow at our colonel the trumpeter attached to the commander's person had levelled him with a pistol-shot. At the same instant Major Bertin and another officer named Maréchal, both of whom had but lately received their promotion, were struck down in death. Two other officers, MM. Roissard and Maille, were grievously wounded by lance-thrusts. In a word, out of thirty officers ten were disabled and two killed outright. It was indeed high time for the young and intrepid Major Hulot to arrive with the 7th Chasseurs. He rushed into the fray with the Salmon and Paravey companies as

soon as they had cleared the bridge. These troops fell like thunder-
bolts upon the enemy's cavalry, sabring, thrusting, and smiting down
everything that opposed their terrific onslaught. Thereupon the 20th
Chasseurs resumed the offensive and the enemy's complete rout was
soon an accomplished fact.

On this occasion I was in charge of a squad of men from the Élite
company and rode straight toward a point where the road turned
sharply to the north, so that I might cut off the retreat of the Uhlans.
Suddenly a Barko hussar, whom I had not noticed galloping behind
me, took aim at me with his pistol from short range. The bullet cut
through the flesh part of my left arm and pierced my coat, close to the
body, traversing my undress cap, which was folded under the coat, and

then going out toward the right side. Feeling that I was badly wounded and losing blood copiously I faced about to retire to the rear.

I had hardly ridden that way as much as fifty feet when I was met by Colonel Castex, who demanded of me:

"Where are you going, sir?"

"I am going to the ambulance to be cared for, Colonel," I answered him, showing where I had been hit, and exhibiting my sabre still wet with the enemy's blood. "You can see, Colonel, that I have been doing my duty."

"Yes, yes," he replied, "I saw you at work, Parquin."

So I withdrew toward the ambulance, which I found on the highway about a league in the rear.

There also I found the black charger, with short-clipped tail and ears, that had belonged to my officer of the Barko Hussars. This was of course my property, since the officer had fallen from his saddle shot dead by my pistol fire. I had lent the horse to a *chasseur* whose mount was disabled. Another charger also belonged to me,—that of a Uhlan I had disabled. This one I had placed in care of a trumpeter named Saron, a boy scarcely twelve years old, who proved not to be hardy enough to continue very long in such a desperate fight and with such gallant and sturdy foes.

When I reached the ambulance the surgeon—noticing how much blood I had lost already and that my coat was cut both on right and left sides—was at first apprehensive that a bullet had pierced me through. In his hurry to discover the truth he even tore off some buttons from my uniform in attempting to throw it open. He at once congratulated me, however, on my fortunate escape, as the bullet had only ploughed the surface flesh instead of penetrating to a mortal or dangerous depth.

In this same fight young Lauriston, who joined the regiment but a few days before, had an encounter with a captain of Uhlans whose horse he overthrew. This officer held up his hands, crying:

"I am your prisoner; I surrender; do not hurt me."

Lauriston had the captain freed from the horse's weight and at once sent him to his father, at headquarters, where the general was acting as *aide-de-camp* to the emperor.

As soon as the prisoner was brought in the courtiers magnified his rank from that of captain into colonel, against whom the whilom page had fought in single combat in the presence of his whole regiment! Thus does it happen that glaring errors find a way into the pages of history, for the incident so distorted to the ears of the emperor was by him put down as fact in a bulletin to the army. The narration is not made here, however, to diminish the fame of Lauriston, who gave repeated proofs of his lofty courage.

In 1814 I chanced to visit General Lauriston, and was gazing intently at a huge painting that depicted this singular duel of his son with a colonel of the Uhlans. My host approached me and said:

"Now, Captain Parquin, you who belong to the 20th chasseurs, pray tell me how far correct you find this painting?"

Although by temperament I am no courtier I was self-possessed enough to answer:

"I must admit, General, that the uniforms are strikingly exact."

By means of this little evasion I managed to get out of the quandary without telling a falsehood.

But let us return to the ambulance, where I found a number of *chasseurs* and several officers wounded.

Among them was a second-lieutenant, Maille by name, who had just come out of the Velites of the Guard, and was now in his first campaign. I said to him; "Should we continue on the high road just now, my dear comrade, we shall be very poorly lodged and probably meet with mishaps. If you agree with me let us both ride toward the right or the left until we find a more suitable resting-place.'"

He accepted my proposal and we rode a few leagues backward toward the left of Amstetten, on the Lintz road. We thus reached the little city of Styer, where we found safe lodging, M. Maille at the vicar's manse and I at the home of the burgomaster. We had taken care to supply ourselves each with an orderly, having chosen two men who were but slightly wounded.

We remained very quiet in this cantonment, where we procured the attendance of a surgeon. It was my host himself who acted in that capacity, for he was the physician and surgeon of the little burg that sheltered us. About a fortnight later we had gained considerable strength and were fairly convalescent, although a couple of weeks more were needful to complete our recovery. One morning, however, the burgomaster, who could speak French, informed us of the Battle of Essling, which he declared to have been a triumph for the Austrian army. I immediately urged on my comrade that we should join the army at once, as in the hour of greatest disaster every officer was bound to be present in the ranks.

"But," objected Maille, "neither of us, my dear Parquin, is yet restored to health."

"Oh, we shall get well enough on the road," I answered determinedly, "and you may be certain in advance that our return will produce an excellent impression."

"That is all very well," said Maille, "But I could n't stand the ride on horseback: that lance-thrust I got in the abdomen would give me infinite torture."

"Is that all? Well, then, use your vicar's buggy. I shall have the mayor call for it by requisition, and you can travel in it at easy stages until you are able to mount again."

"Well, I'll try it," said Maille, "if only you will wait a week longer."

"All right; agreed that we shall start on the 1st of June."

In accordance with our compact we set out on that day, my friend Maille in the vicar's carriage and I on horseback, for I could endure the riding by keeping my arm bound close to my side. The next day we entered on the Vienna high road and passed over the very spot where we had been wounded and where so many of our comrades had been laid in the earth—over the very ground where our brigade had covered itself with glory. On June 3rd we entered Vienna and there learned that our command had left the city on May 11th, with the cavalry of the Montbrun division, which formed the vanguard of General Lauriston's army corps. Our troops were to effect a junc-

tion with the viceroy at Neustadt, where His Majesty had driven the retreating army of Archduke John.

We stopped for some time in Vienna. There I met an infantry officer of the Imperial Guard, whose family, while living at Joigny, had been intimate with my own people. Hospitality being thus incumbent on me, I invited him to dinner. He belonged to General Michel's division, which had been reviewed the same morning at

Schoenbrunn, on its arrival from France. The general was greatly worried thinking of the reception he would surely have from the emperor, he being one day overdue in the march. Here is how this officer himself related the incident to me:

"You must understand, my dear Parquin, that a division of grenadiers both from the Young and Old Guards, is a resource on which the emperor counts, and it must be available on the very day fixed by him. General Michel, when he left barracks at the Paris Military School, received orders to join the emperor on June 1st. All the stages had been laid out in advance, and the general firmly believed that no human power, except a clear command of the emperor, could possibly delay him one hour. It so happened, however, that on the day

132

the regiment reached Stuttgart, the King of Wurtemberg, who very cordially welcomed the general and his officers, when they called upon him as in duty bound, announced his intention to review the division next morning. The general excused himself, saying that he had formal orders from the emperor to reach Schoenbrunn on June 1st, and that his hours were measured.

"'I shall review your troops. General,'" retorted the king, 'or I will see to it that you receive neither supplies, nor lodgings, nor wagons for your transport.'"

"To the indignant protests of the general, the king simply answered: "'I believe I am the master here and you may be sure that I will act as I say.'

"General Michel might have answered the king: 'Sire, with my

133

division I need have no trouble obtaining supplies anywhere, even if I have to take possession of your whole kingdom,' but he preferred to say:

"'Your Majesty's arguments are such that I have only to bow before them. At what hour will it please Your Majesty to review my division?'

"'At noon,' answered the king as he dismissed us.

"On the same day. General Michel sent a courier ahead to notify the major-general of the event that would delay his arrival one day.

"Next morning we were reviewed by the King of Wurtemberg. Seated in an open barouche. His Majesty displayed his enormous paunch and caused our troops no little merriment when they discovered his method of reviewing regiments.

"The same evening the officers were invited to dinner at the palace, and His Majesty was kind enough to compliment us upon the fine bearing of our division. He even added that he had now seen the most valiant soldiers in the world.

"We left Stuttgart the next morning, but of course this incident caused us to reach Schoenbrunn one day later than prescribed.

"The emperor, who had been notified of the facts, remarked to the Prince of Neufchâtel, in the presence of General Michel:

"'If that man [speaking of the King of Wurtemberg] were only thirty years younger, and could manage to melt in a day about two hundred pounds of useless fat, I would appoint him my major-general, for he has lots of energy.'"

On the 5th we readied Œdenburg, a small Hungarian city. So far my friend Maille had stood the journey fairly well; but such was not the case with me, for the extreme heat had inflamed my wound and my arm began to swell painfully. On reaching my quarters, I sent for a doctor, who, after examining my arm, expressed much surprise that I should have started before my wound was properly closed and added that gangrene might set in if I persisted riding on in the hottest month of the year. His opinion settled the matter. I allowed my friend to continue the trip alone while I began to bestow on myself the proper nursing. The surgeon had told me that within three weeks I should be perfectly well again. I no longer hesitated to spend so much time in this little place, especially as I had conceived great faith in the surgeon I met thus by chance.

I was barely two days in Œdenburg when I received a most unexpected visit. The burgomaster and two of the city council came to my

rooms and on my asking them to what I was indebted for the honour of their call, the burgomaster said:

"Sir, when the city of Œdenburg was first occupied by your troops, an army corps commanded by General Lauriston was quartered within our limits. When the general departed he neglected to leave behind an officer to take military charge of the place, and the consequence is that we have much trouble with stragglers who pass through the city on the way to their regiments, and who are often very ugly customers to deal with. There is no French authority here that can impress them with any respect, and on that account we come to you, sir, to ask, as a special favour, that you take command of our city until your arm be perfectly cured. The doctor who attends to you is one of our aldermen, and he states that you may be kept among us for at least three weeks. We shall feel deeply grateful, sir, if you will comply with our request."

"I am pleased to accept your offer," I answered, "and I do so in the interest of my compatriots as much as in yours; but remember that no consideration whatever will induce me to remain here one day longer than is needed to accomplish my cure."

Next morning I had a sentry on duty at my door, with a picket of four men and a corporal from the civic guard at my disposal. I at once entered on my self-assumed duties as military commander of Œdenburg. I had only accepted the dignity just two days, when a party of infantry officers reached the place. They were the bodyguard of the viceroy on their way to join his army. I provided officers' quarters for them, to which they were fully entitled, but I had the greatest trouble in making the municipal authorities recognize that these gentlemen were not common soldiers, although their uniforms were covered with braiding both front and back.

On the 10th of June arrived a courier from the major-general, bearer of despatches for General Marmont, who was then at Laybach in Illyria. I had no means of transmitting these despatches onward, for the road to Italy was infested by stray parties of General Chasteler's cavalry, detached from Archduke John's army to worry the viceroy's rear. I was very desirous, however, of having the despatches reach General Marmont, since his movements must certainly be of importance under the circumstances. The major-general's courier was well aware of the dangers that pervaded the route, and declined to proceed further than Œdenburg on his errand, transferring to my charge the parcel from the major-general. It was then about ten o'clock in the evening. I had the municipal council at once called in special session at the City Hall, the burgomaster presiding, and I made them the following speech:

"Gentlemen, I am in possession of despatches which must, by some means or other, reach General Marmont at Laybach in Illyria. I wish you to select for me an intelligent citizen, speaking sufficient French, an acquirement which is not unusual in your city. He must be provided with a good post-chaise and a servant. You will also get him a passport describing him as a Hungarian nobleman on a visit to Illyria for his health. Should he meet on the road some of the scouts of general Chasteler he will have only to show his passport to be readily allowed to proceed, for the Austrian troops have no motive to inconvenience their compatriots. If, on the contrary, he meet French troops, he will hand over to them the parcel addressed to General Marmont, and his mission will then be successfully ended. What do we need, gentlemen,

to make the whole thing a success? Only an intelligent Hungarian, a post-chaise, a passport, and sufficient money. Here is the parcel of despatches, which I place in the burgomaster's hands, and for which I shall take his receipt. Let me add, gentlemen, that if the affair is not carried out in accordance with my requirements, I shall take care to have the emperor at once informed of your neglect and you may rely on it that your city will have to pay him a stiff contribution."

The council discussed the matter for a few moments, *pro forma*, and finally acceded to my plan. Within a week the messenger returned, bringing a receipt from General Marmont, whom he had found at the head of his army corps a few miles beyond Laybach. He handed me, besides, a package addressed to the major-general, and which I placed in the care of the original messenger to take back to headquarters.

On June 15th a courier from the emperor's household reached the city, bringing me a letter addressed to "The *Commandant* of the City of Œdenburg, in Hungary." This letter was penned, from the first to the last word, in the handwriting of the emperor. It was of course illegible, but General Lemarrois, his *aide-de-camp*, had transcribed it beneath in a very fair hand. Here is the letter:

"*Commandant;*—General Chasteler, with a corps of Austrian cavalry, has taken a post of observation on the rear of the Italian army. The Polish Light-Horse regiment of my Guard will soon arrive to garrison Œdenburg. Take such measures, in accord with its colonel, as will prevent the road between your city and Comorn from being obstructed and hold yourself on the *qui-vive.*

"Napoleon."

"Shoenbrunnn. June 15th, 1809."

Next morning as announced the regiment of Light Horse came in. Forage, supplies and quarters were ready for them. I at once called upon General Krasinski, the colonel of the regiment, and informed him of the contents of the emperor's letter, which he persuaded me to leave in his possession as it concerned the service of his regiment.

During the stay of the lancers at Œdenburg I contracted an intimacy with their adjutant-major, M. Duvivier. He was the only Frenchman belonging to this corps.

On the 14th of June, the anniversary of Marengo and of Friedland, Prince Eugene gained the victory of Raab over Archduke John and the Archduke Palatine, who had joined his brother at Comorn with six thousand raw Hungarian recruits. The result of the battle was a complete rout of the Austrians, who lost a number of men, several cannon and standards, and between five and six thousand prisoners.

On the 16th of June a party of wounded men from the 20th Chasseurs reached Œdenburg, among them being Corporal André, from whom I sought some news concerning my old regiment.

"We have had terrible losses," he informed me, "especially in the Élite company; Captain Capitan and Second-Lieutenant Henri have both died from their wounds."

These last words brought the tears to my eyes: "What?—my poor Henri!" I cried out. "Did his death come to him mercifully?"

"I saw him fall from his horse, struck by a cannonball that carried off his leg. We took him over to the ambulance, and the same evening the company was informed that he died a few minutes after enduring, with supreme fortitude, the amputation of his shattered limb."

"Captain Capitan," added André, "was even more unfortunate, for he was, so to speak, directed to his death by those who wished to save him. I'll tell you how it happened. It was about seven o'clock in the evening and firing had ceased along the whole line. I almost think that the ball which struck the captain was the very last shot the enemy fired that night. M. Capitan had just dismounted, and was passing the bridle of his horse to one of the troopers, walked off a few paces.

"He then stood awhile talking, and looking toward the enemy, when the mounted *chasseurs* noticed a cannonball bounding straight toward him. At once they shouted, all together: "Look out. captain; look out! There's a cannonball plunging toward you!" Hearing this warning, the

captain, by an involuntary movement, drew back his right leg that was poised a little ahead, and just at that very second it was struck by the ball and smashed into pieces. A few minutes later he was dead."

I sincerely regretted the captain, but I need hardly say that just at that moment my grief at the loss of dear Henri was paramount to all.

On June 20th I received from the headquarters of the Prince of Neufchâtel a bundle of printed handbills, to be posted or distributed throughout the city of Œdenburg. The object of the proclamation was to shake the allegiance of the Hungarians toward the Imperial court of Austria, this sentiment having shown itself much more tenacious than anyone would conceive possible. I remember that in the document Emperor Napoleon addressed these words to them, which certainly seemed persuasive enough to uproot their loyalty to the Austrian crown:

"I want nothing from you, Hungarians. You have a language of your own. Become a nation again; assemble once more on the white

plains of Racos, as your forefathers did of old, and there, according to your ancient custom, elect your own chief and king. I will accept him at your hands."

But the Hungarians remained immovably attached to their sovereign. Every copy of the proclamation, printed both in Latin and German, that we posted up in the evening was torn to pieces during the night. I had now been three weeks at Œdenburg and my wound was as well as could be expected, so I decided on writing the following letter to the Prince of Neufchâtel:

"Prince:

"The city of Œdenburg, Hungary, has been left since the passage of General Lauriston's army corps without a military commander. As I was riding through the place to join my regiment, a wound that I had received on the 6th of May, and which I considered almost healed, again became troublesome and compelled me to stop for a rest.

"The burgomaster and two aldermen thereupon came forward and begged me to assume military command of their city. I accepted the situation, as it allowed me, in spite of my wound, to be still in active service and to be helpful to the army in the post thus offered me. I am now entirely cured and it is my duty to join my regiment. I therefore humbly request Your Serene Highness to despatch an officer to assume the duties of commandant at this place, which, on account of the resources it contains, deserves to be properly cared for.

"I have the honour to be, Prince, with the deepest respect,

"Your very humble and obedient servant,

"Ch. Parquin.

"Œdenburg,

"June 24th, 1809

"Second-Lieutenant in the 20th Chasseurs

"Now Military-Commandant of the City of Œdenburg."

On the 20th of June a major from the general staff reached Œdenburg, having orders signed by the Prince of Neufchâtel appointing him military commander of the city. He was instructed to collect all needed information from Lieutenant Parquin, concerning his new duties, and to authorize that officer to return to his regiment if his wound were sufficiently healed.

The next day I finally left Œdenburg, bearing with me, I am pleased to say, the esteem of the worthy citizens. I joined my regiment at its bivouac, close to the Danube bridge. I was delighted to he once more with my comrades, and they welcomed me very

pleasantly, but I was saddened to the depths of my heart not to find among them my dear friend Henri.

I learned a few details concerning his death. Sergeant Nicloux, who had been charged with the care of my wounded friend as far as the ambulance, told me that when the amputation was over he laboured hard to reassure Henri as to the probable results, saying to him:

"Only think, Lieutenant, in a few months you will be sheltered at the Palais des Invalides, and will be sketching out battle-plans with your cane on the garden walks."

"I thus tried to distract his mind from the gravity of his condition," added Nicloux, "for I was very much afraid lest a spell of fever,

the natural outcome of such a terrible operation, should suddenly carry off my worthy lieutenant. I was much distressed on this point but managed to conceal my fears. Suddenly, the lieutenant said to me: 'Sergeant, give me my leather pouch.'

"Handing it to him at once I noticed he drew out of the pouch a small looking-glass, which he had always used for his toilet in the bivouac and even on the march—for the dear gentleman was rather proud of his good looks. After glancing into it briefly he said to me, the while pressing my hand:

"Goodbye, sergeant; many thanks for your attentions; give the assurance of my friendship to all comrades, the present and the absent.

[I understood what was meant by these words, for Henri and I were greatly attached to each other.] Tell them that I am proud of myself, for I look death in the face without flinching.'

"Just one minute later our brave lieutenant breathed his last. His death caused general grief in the regiment."

On July 5th we rode out to a village about three leagues this side of the Wagram bridge; there we bivouacked. That night, while sleeping on the straw with my comrades, under the roof of a deserted farmhouse, I awoke at midnight and observed an officer named Rhault very busy writing letters:

"What are you scribbling at so late, my dear comrade?" I asked him.

"I am writing to my people [he was originally from Verdun] and also to a young lady whom I have loved for a long time, who loves me

in return, and to whom I am engaged. I am telling them that tomorrow, in the battle we are now expecting, I shall be among the slain."

"Oh, it is only a nightmare you have," I exclaimed, "and you know that dreams always turn out contrary."

Again I stretched out on the straw and slept soundly until five o'clock; at that hour the trumpeters were rousing the whole bivouac and shortly afterward I was myself in the saddle.

On that day, July 6th, the sun had hardly time to light up the horizon, when a forest of bayonets was glittering all over the plain, reflecting his rays in a thousand different directions. Drums were heard beating on all sides; everything seemed to foretell a warm and interesting day. Our brigade had ridden forward to take its place as the vanguard of the grenadiers under command of General Oudinot. From eight

o'clock in the morning we manoeuvred under fire of the enemy's artillery. It was noon when General Colbert's brigade, nine squadrons strong, to which our regiment belonged, was moved forward by squadrons at the trot and took ground in the centre of the army, just behind one hundred guns of the artillery of the Imperial Guard, commanded by General Lauriston. We were quite within range of the enemy's artillery, which held a most formidable position and were

returning our people's fire. The gunners of the Guard had stripped off their coats to be more free in movement.

Lieutenant Lauriston was in command of a squad of horse next to mine. His father, who was in command of the entire artillery of the Guard, came over every half hour to chat awhile with the younger officer. Hardly a minute had elapsed since he last left him when a cannonball pierced Lauriston's horse through and through. The missile

grazed the left calf of the rider and came out behind his right calf. He of course fell under his horse, and for a moment I feared that one or both of his legs had been carried off. I ordered several *chasseurs* to dismount and pull him from under his dead charger, while I asked:

"Lauriston, is your left leg hit?"

He answered me:

"I hardly feel it at all, dear Parquin, it is so terribly benumbed."

At length the *chasseurs* managed to lift him out of his painful position, but our anxiety vanished when we saw him spring to his feet.

"There is nothing the matter with me," he cried, "I have not even been touched."

"Well, if that's so, my dear fellow," I replied, "allow me to congratulate you; you have had a pretty narrow escape."

Lauriston walked on a.few yards until he found one of his father's horses, for none of our spare mounts had been allowed to cross the river, orders having been given to permit only the fighting men to pass the bridge and to leave the orderlies and extra horses behind.

Half an hour later I noticed General Lauriston approaching us, doubtless to hear news about his son. I sent one of my corporals to meet him and to reassure him as to the outcome of this adventure.

We had been a full hour in this awkward but honourable position—for we were covering one hundred cannon of the Guard against the possibility of an attack from the enemy's cavalry—when at last our firing silenced Prince Charles' guns. Only then did our brigade start forward, resuming the same road and riding in the same order as before. Farther along we could see the cannonballs that had passed through or over our ranks and fallen close to the emperor, in front of whose *cortège* we were now filing. Before reaching our position on the battlefield, in front of the grenadiers, we crossed a stream of some volume that babbled through the plain of Wagram. At about two o'clock we were formed in battle array. Before us in the open space lay three Austrian infantry squares, six ranks deep, commanded by the Prince of Hohenzollern.

Lieutenant Lauriston had joined us in great haste, astride one of his father's chargers and without having taken time to substitute his regimental housings for the gold-braided trappings of his new mount.

At this moment General Oudinot galloped in front of our brigade, calling out to Colonel Labiffe, whom he well knew:

"Pick yourself up, Labiffe, you are about to charge!"

A second later General Colbert shouted to his brigade, giving the

order to the 7th Chasseurs and 9th Hussars to "Charge" and to smite the enemy's squares just facing them.

The 7th Chasseurs charged with their usual vigour, General Colbert being at the front, but had not advanced over a hundred feet when a terrible fusillade from the enemy's squares wrought wide havoc in their ranks. General Colbert was shot in the head, several officers were killed or wounded, and fifty or sixty *chasseurs* bit the dust. The 7th was compelled to retreat. Seeing this, Colonel Castex, instead of charging the square opposite him, as he had been ordered to do, decided to throw his regiment, which was still at the trot, against the square that had so thoroughly repulsed the chasseurs. He commanded in his stentorian voice:

"Squadrons! to the right! Gallop! Charge!"

The square could not resist this fresh onslaught and was utterly broken. The 9th Hussars had gallantly carried their square; thus the brigade had succeeded in crushing two out of three squares, under a galling fire from the artillery of the enemy, who were now raining grape-shot into our ranks and even into those of their own captured infantry.

Lieutenant Lauriston had hardly joined us when a cannonball killed the horse he recently mounted, so his father said to him the same evening:

"It were better had you taken my poorest instead of my best charger, since you were plainly resolved on its being killed right away."

In the square we had broken into my horse was wounded by a bayonet-thrust in the left shoulder, and as I led him away, limping, I met, on his way to the ambulance, Lieutenant Rhault, who had prophesied his own death the night before. He had only received a slight wound in the thigh.

"Well, lieutenant," I said to him smiling, "you see how absurd it is to believe in presentiments!"

"That's so," he replied. "I got off pretty cheap: I did wrong to write to my folks as I did."

He had hardly uttered the words when a small shell from the enemy's battery struck him on the helmet, crashed into his skull and laid him out stone dead. I related to Colonel Castex this sad occurrence, as well as the strange fact of poor Rhault having had such fate. The letter he had written to his people the previous night was taken back from the regimental post-office, and the colonel wrote instead an official advice to the family, stating that this officer had been wounded and succumbed after a week in the hospital.

At half-past three the Battle of Wagram was over, so far as our brigade was concerned, though along toward the left Masséna's corps kept fighting until the stroke of midnight. Our regiment bivouacked on the very spot where we had charged those two infantry squares of Hohenzollern's division, and where we captured a batch of two thousand prisoners. The victory of Wagram, which Prince Charles disputed with us so sturdily, gave us in all twenty thousand prisoners, a number of flags, and thirty cannon; so you see that our brigade earned its full share of the general triumph.

On that day our army lost the intrepid General Lasalle. He also, the same morning had predicted what his fate would be. His war-horse, which an orderly had foolishly led in the early morning to a stream beyond the outposts, was seized together with the orderly by one of the enemy's scouting parties. This was the first mishap of which the general was that day a victim. A little later, while rummaging through one of the holsters on the horse he had mounted, in search of a small brandy-flask which he had ordered his servant to place there, he found in its stead only the fragments of the broken glass.

"Nothing is going right today," he exclaimed, "I feel certain that I am to be killed."

Two hours afterward he was mortally wounded in a brilliant charge, which he himself led against the enemy's squares, falling at the head of the squadrons he had so often cheered to victory.

Major Daumesnil and Major Corbineau of the *chasseurs* of the Imperial Guard each lost a limb. Everyone knows how the emperor rewarded these two devoted officers. To General Daumesnil he gave command of the fortress of Vincennes, where this valiant officer later added to his renown, by his reply to the victorious Allies when they entered Paris, on being called upon to surrender:

"Inform the enemy that when they have returned me my absent leg I shall surrender the keys of this fortress. Until then let them keep out of range of my shells—or else suffer the consequences."

It was the same Daumesnil who, when a, private at St. Jean d'Acre, in the escort squadron of General Bonaparte, freely risked his life to save that of his general. On the occasion referred to he stood close behind the general-in chief and Berthier, holding their horses and his own, when a shell dropped to the earth only four feet away from the group. Realizing at once the danger his general was exposed to, Daumesnil did not hesitate a, single instant; he left the horses and running toward his chief placed himself bodily between the general and the projectile about to explode. Most luckily the shell went so deep into the sand that it did not burst, whereupon Daumesnil returned to his horses. General Bonaparte, whose eagle glance had taken in the whole incident, silent though it had been, spoke only three words, but words more eloquent than all the praise in the world:

"What a soldier!"

General Corbineau awaited the emperor's return to Paris before asking for his reward. At that time the treasuryship of Rouen had become vacant, and the officer respectfully begged his sovereign to appoint him to the vacant position.

"And who will furnish your bond?" said the emperor.

"My leg, Sire, will be my bond."

"And I suppose that I shall also have to sign the bond," said the emperor, smiling; and he granted General Corbineau's appointment.

Being desirous to choose himself, among the colonels of the army, an officer for the rank of major of his Guide, the emperor had Marshal Bessières present to him a list of candidates, at the bottom of which Colonel Lion's name was inscribed. His Majesty read the list through, and having noticed the last name on it, said:

"I need a *lion* to be major in such a regiment," and the colonel of the 14th Chasseurs was promoted into the Guard *chasseurs*.

It was during the Battle of Wagram that the regiment of Light Horse of the Guard, which had visited Œdenburg during my stay there, had its famous and bloody encounter with a regiment of the enemy's lancers. The Light Horse worsted their opponents by dint of sabre cuts and carbine blows, and then seized on the enemy's lances, the favourite weapon of the Poles, with which to finish their gory task. Later in the day, and while still armed with the lances, they attacked and dispersed the regiment of Latour Dragoons, which held in the Austrian Army a like position to that of our regiments of horse *carbineers*. When Marshal Bessières informed the emperor, the same evening, of the splendid work of his Light Horse cavalry. His Majesty said:

"Let them be given lances, since they know so well how to use them." On the morning after the Battle of Wagram the army was notified, in the order of the day, that the emperor had created Macdonald, Oudinot and Marmont marshals of France. The French soldier, with his keen spirit of epigram, spoke of the new marshals in this wise:

"France has appointed Macdonald, the Army has chosen Oudinot, Friendship has promoted Marmont."

From the 7th to the 10th of July our brigade, deprived of its general, who had retired to Vienna because of a shot-wound in the head, manoeuvred under the orders of Colonel Gauthrin, commander of the 9th Hussars. On the 10th we were incorporated with General Montbrun's division, and rode as far as the city of Zuaim, where we came upon the united army of the enemy formed in battle array. We assumed the general attack to be imminent. Already Masséna's corps with that of Marshal Oudinot had reached the suburbs of Zuaim, and we could hear the thunder of artillery, when, about seven o'clock, the bearer of a flag of truce presented himself at our outposts, asking free passage for Prince Lichtenstein on his way to the emperor to beg for a suspension of hostilities. The armistice was concluded on the 18th of July. It was to last for one month subject to fifteen days notice by either party. This allowed the army, and especially our brigade, to secure excellent cantonments in Moravia until the final treaty of peace. I had my quarters and those of my squad in a beautiful village close to a great castle belonging to Prince Esterhazy. I mustered the command in parade on the church square to distribute the men's billets, which the first sergeant had procured, when this non-commissioned officer handed me my own billet. I was surprised to discover that I was to

take up quarters at the house of the village priest and not at the castle. The sergeant, to whom I sharply expressed my vexation, said to me:

"I thought, lieutenant, that you would find yourself more comfortable in a house occupied by its owner, than in a castle from which the prince is absent, there being merely an overseer in charge."

A feeling of excusable vanity made me wish to date my letter from Prince Esterhazy's castle rather than from the village manse. Accordingly I soon rode over there, when the overseer at once came to welcome me and assured me that he would obey whatever orders I chose to give. He further told me that the wine-cellar was abundantly stocked, and in fact he seemed desirous to meet my every wish. Thereupon I invited the first sergeant to dine with me every day, so as not to be quite exclusive in my stately privileges.

But I was not to be left long alone in my *château*. I had barely been there a few days when General Piré, his *aide-de-camp*, the regimental staff of the 16th Horse Chasseurs and the Élite company of the same regiment rode into the village and occupied it. The general had been permitted by Colonel Castex, who was not under his orders, to enter our cantonments, and even to take up quarters in the *château*, provided, of course, that he should not displace the officer and twenty-seven *chasseurs* of the 20th who were already in possession of those comfortable lodgings. I at once tendered General Piré my own room, which he accepted, but on condition that I should accept next choice and would likewise take all my meals at his table—a stipulation to which I gratefully assented.

Lieutenant Castelbajac was the general's *aide-de-camp*, and his assistant was Lieutenant Guindey of the 10th Hussars, whose friend I had been for years. He was the same officer who, in the campaign of 1806, had slain Prince Louis of Prussia at Saalfeld.

When everybody was comfortably fixed in village and *château* you should have seen the demeanour of His Excellency's overseer—instead of being at all worried he showed himself positively delighted. Rubbing his hands cheerily he would say to me:

"I tell you, lieutenant, that Prince Esterhazy is rightly honoured! It is really worthwhile to be entertaining such guests, who know what a good thing is, and especially General Piré, who has such an excellent cook of his own. I assure you, sir, I should have been ashamed, when my lord returns, if I could not lay before him a bill for your entertainment of at least ten florins a day."

"So your prince is very rich, I understand?"

159

"Rich!" exclaimed the overseer, "don't you know the fortune of Prince Esterhazy?"

"I have not the faintest idea; nevertheless his name is not quite new to me, for before the Revolution one of our French regiments, I think the 3rd Hussars, used to be called the Esterhazy Regiment."

"I believe," resumed the overseer, "that my master is the richest prince in Europe. Besides the diamonds he owns, which are worth a vast amount of money, his domains, and especially those in Austria-Hungary, are so extensive as to afford grazing land for over ten thousand sheep!"

Twenty years after the time I now refer to, Madame Parquin and myself had the honour of receiving a visit from Prince Esterhazy at the Wolffsburg Château. This nobleman had come over to purchase the *château* of the island of Mainau, in Lake Constance, a few leagues from Wolffsburg. At that period the prince was still a well-preserved man and a splendid rider; nor ever wanting in a gallant speech when addressing the lady he escorted. It is seldom one meets in society a gentleman of loftier breeding; he was indeed among the last of those nobles of the old *régime* of whom M. de Talleyrand, in France, had been one of the most distinguished types.

I was told at the time by a well informed person that the fortune

161

of Prince Esterhazy had been assigned to a committee of trustees, that is, a family-council had taken charge of the estates. I should never have imagined that such an event could ensue when I was listening to the magnificent descriptions of his Moravian overseer. But let us return to our cantonments.

The general was fond of good living, was a typical soldier and very kind to young people. We were told that during the Prussian campaign of 1806, when he was still but captain in a hussar regiment, he had one night to surprise Graudentz, a fortified city then in the hands of the enemy. This gallant feat was made possible because the majority of his soldiers spoke German fluently. Having levied an immediate and heavy contribution he abandoned the place again at dawn of day, at the head of his regiment, leaving the enemy perfectly astounded by the daring of his performance.

At the castle we had regular *déjeûner* every morning at ten; at five o'clock we enjoyed a two-course dinner with dessert, coffee and liquors. In the building was an excellent billiard table to help while away the time and the dice or playing cards were always to be found on the tables reserved for them. On the 15th of August the hunting season began, and we did not fail to make the most of our opportunity. The general was a keen sportsman, and when we went for a regular chase we invariably returned to the *château* with large quantities of game, an exploit which tickled the overseer immensely, as being a token of what he liked to call the "princely splendour" of his master.

One morning, being weary with shooting hares, partridges and foxes, Castelbajac and Guindey made a wager as to which could bring down the greater number of swallows. After a full quarter of an hour they hadn't shot even one. They were chaffing each other about the poor marksmanship when Guindey, eager to prove his merits as a crack shot, offered to shoot at Castelbajac from one hundred paces, engaging merely to "flesh" him above the knee joint. He pledged himself, in case of failure, to offer himself as a target under the same conditions. They were both very hare-brained fellows indeed, for the

wager was not only proposed but accepted, and they had already taken places and were aiming when I interposed and said to Guindey:

"My dear fellow, I have no objection to your trying each other's skill at your own expense, but before you begin I would beg you to kindly return me the trousers I have lent you, and which I don't care to see spoiled!"

My request, made with great gravity, put an end to the absurd contest, which might have resulted in a most unpleasant manner. On December 15th General Colbert, having recovered from his wound, assembled his brigade on a plateau close to the Brunn highway to be reviewed by the emperor. It was a fine day in the early autumn. The brigade was formed up in three lines, consisting respectively of the 9th Hussars, the 7th and the 20th Chasseurs. The emperor arrived at twelve o'clock sharp, and riding slowly along the front of the columns appeared to be satisfied and gave orders for a few promotions and decorations. He never allowed the latter to exceed twelve for each regiment during any one campaign.

Colonel Castex was made commander of the Legion of Honour, and received, a few days later, his brevet of brigadier-general. Our two majors were granted their pensions. MM. Curély and de Vérigny, captains of the 6th and 7th Hussars respectively, were promoted to their places. They were both excellent officers as the reader will see farther on. Lieutenants Lacour and Lauriston were each promoted to a captaincy. Among the officers who received the cross of the Legion was my good friend Maille, whose visage, instead of being soldierly, was more like the countenance of a timid clerk.

This characteristic of the gallant officer proved somewhat like an omen of his future peaceful career, for I found him, thirty years later, officiating as mayor of the small provincial town of Doullens, performing his duties as chief of the municipality to the great satisfaction of citizens. On that particular day the emperor, who could see nothing warlike in his face, observed to the colonel, who was introducing M. Maille to him as an officer who had been wounded during the Uhlan's charge:

"Wounded, wounded; that is a rather poor reason for his being decorated; has he inflicted any wounds among the enemy?"

"Sire, this officer has done his full duty."

And M. Maille received the cross.

The colonel presented also to the emperor, as entitled to a cross, the paymaster of the regiment. Either because his name seemed very incongruous with any act of bravery (he was called Jean Jean) or from some other motive, the emperor answered, while rubbing his thumb and fingertips together in a significant way:

"Oh, a paymaster always rewards himself like this."

But as the colonel persisted in stating that this officer had rendered very material services to the regiment for four years past, the emperor, to dispose of the matter, inquired:

"I suppose he can handle a squad properly?"

The colonel answered affirmatively, although the fact was at least dubious. Jean Jean received his cross.

The review ended in our "riding by" at full gallop in squadrons, with shouts of "Long live the Emperor!"

The emperor concluded the inspection by ordering the colonel to provide cloth trousers after the first of October. We had gone through the whole campaign wearing duck trousers.

We returned to our cantonments; but early in November the army began its retrograde movement. About the same time Major Cavrois, of the Guard *chasseurs*, was appointed colonel of our regiment in place of Colonel Castex, promoted to brigadier-general. We set out on our march from the hereditary states of Austria to occupy a position in Bavaria. On February 10th, 1810, we left Bavaria for France and on the 1st of March reached Strasburg. General Castex, who had been married and was now living in Strasburg, came over with General Colbert to Kehl to review our regiment. The corps of officers gave a dinner to the two generals at the Maison-Rouge Hotel in Strasburg. It was on

that day I made the acquaintance of MM. Bro and de Brack, *aides-de-camp* to General Colbert. The latter of these gentlemen had received the nickname of Miss de Brack, not because of his deficiency in any military qualities, for he had, on the contrary, the reputation of being a very fine soldier and a capital officer; but his youth, the whiteness of his skin, his golden hair, the absence of any beard, and the slenderness of his figure, had brought about the bestowal of this fancy sobriquet.

I had at this time been away from France about four years, having passed the Rhine at Mayence in 1806 and recrossed it by the Strasburg bridge in 1810. During the four years—I hope I may be allowed to remind the reader of this—I had gone through the Prussian campaign of 1806 and through the Eylau campaign of 1807, until I was wounded and made prisoner; finally, through the campaign of 1809, where I was wounded by a gunshot in the right arm. I may add, using the words of the emperor, that if I was wounded I had also wounded others. And yet, the only reward I was bringing home, for seven years' service, was my humble second-lieutenant's epaulet. But those were times of personal abnegation, when one's ambition was fully satisfied in being privileged to fight and vanquish the enemy of the fatherland, and thus conserve for France her title of *The Great Nation*. It fully sufficed that the emperor should appreciate our sleepless nights, our toils and our many wounds, by addressing us the few words:

"Soldiers, I am pleased with you; you have surpassed my expectations!"

And after all, in 1810, though scarcely twenty-three years old, I was both happy and proud, for was I not a French officer?

During the first week of March the Colbert brigade started on its return, being divided into squads of fifty men each under command of an officer, and each distant from the next about as one post-office from another. The brigade was thus extended from Strasburg all the way to Compiègne, for we were also to serve as an escort for the new empress, Marie Louise of Austria. I halted my squad, according to instructions, at Saverne, a small city and sub-prefecture in Lorraine. My orders were to escort the imperial carriages on the main road, but to walk our horses quietly in cities and villages, so as to allow the people to come alongside the vehicles and have a good look at the empress, His Excellency the Prince of Neufchâtel, who had solemnly espoused in Vienna, in the name of Emperor Napoleon, this daughter of the Caesars, directed the march of the *cortège*, having under his orders General Lauriston, *aide-de-camp* to the emperor, who travelled in the prince's carriage. The sixth carriage contained the empress, and by her side, on the left, sat the Queen of Naples.

General Colbert had been appointed equerry to the empress; but instead of riding always on the right of the imperial carriage he would frequently lag behind, appearing to be very tired from the rapid travelling. To this circumstance I owed the gift of an orange, which the empress handed out through the open window, and which I took from her fingers while she was looking around for the absent chamberlain.

The general had requested the officers of the brigade to lend him, at each relay, one of their own horses, kept ready saddled. At Sarreburg, accordingly, my orderly held in readiness the horse that had belonged to the Barko officer, and which 'was now my property. This steed had short ears and tail and was far from being young and stylish. It had a very pleasant gait for its rider, however, being a kind of swing gallop, persistent and regular, to which as a hunter it had been trained for a long time. Having reached Blamont, which ended my relay, General Colbert told me that this horse had proved such a relief to his physical weariness, that he would thank me very much if I allowed him to use it for another stage. Of course I was only too happy to concede this slight favour to the general, with whom I was most anxious to remain on excellent terms.

At Blamont I transmitted the order of march to my friend Jouglas, the officer who was to command the escort during the next stage.

As I stated above these arrangements had given me a chance of surveying quite closely the Empress Marie Louise. She seemed to me a very handsome woman, with a shapely figure, a fresh complexion, beautiful teeth, and a pretty hand, a sure token of a dainty foot. The Queen of Naples, who accompanied her, was then in all the splendour

of her extraordinary beauty.

At the Blamont relay, after the stereotyped welcome of the mayor, a villager, who seemed in good circumstances, for he sported a three-cornered hat, approached the empress' carriage and taking off his head-gear, said to her:

"*Madame*, may you make our great emperor a happy man and bear him plenty of children."

He finished his harangue with shouts of "Long live the Empress Marie Louise! Long live Emperor Napoleon!"

Marie Louise could not help smiling at the Lorraine peasant's unconventional speech, and turning toward the Queen of Naples, she said:

"There is a Frenchman who seems to be quite in a hurry! He should at least wait until I am married."

The cortege proceeded on its way the same evening. Wherever it stopped, in obedience to the empress' orders, she never failed to receive a letter from her august spouse.

General Colbert had returned to me, through my friend Jouglas, the horse I lent him, conveying besides his heartfelt thanks. A few days later I received a letter from the general from Lunéville, in which he requested me to forward to the Lunéville barracks the horse he had borrowed and to name its price. I hastened to obey this order and notified the general that my price would be fifteen *louis* of twenty-four *francs*. I was somewhat pleased to be rid of the horse, for in France,

during a time of peace, I was only entitled to rations for one charger. A week later General Colbert sent me, as the price of my horse, thirty instead of fifteen *louis*. I afterward heard from him that he sold it to the Prince of Neufchâtel, who used it for a hunter on his Grosbois estate. The general added that he had never been so much pleased with the gait of any horse.

On April 10th, 1810, our regiment was garrisoned at Nancy, a city which would be unrivalled for a cavalryman to dwell in if only the barrack stables were a little more decent. We remained there twenty days and left on the 1st of May for Nantes.

CHAPTER 3

Spain
1810-1812

 ate on the 1st of July a despatch from the war department reached Nantes, commanding six hundred cavalry to start for Spain with Major Vérigny at their head. I did not belong to the war squadrons that were thus to enter on campaign again, but as Adjutant-Major Vincent had suddenly fallen ill I was directed to assume his place. I at once purchased an excellent horse that had belonged to Major Curély, who was to remain at Nantes with the regimental *dépôt*, and I set out on my way July 5th, twenty-four hours ahead of the detachment, for which I had to secure provisions, forage and quarters. It was during this march, and while passing through Bordeaux, where we had a brief stop, that I made the acquaintance of Marshal Oudinot's son, who dined with Major de Vérigny, Lauriston and myself. Captain Oudinot was previously a lieutenant in the 5th Hussars, and was now on his way to join Prince Masséna, whose *aide-de-camp* he had been appointed.

We continued our march as far as Bayonne, and crossed the Bidassoa so as to enter Spain by the Irun high road. On the 14th of August we reached Vittoria, where we were at once absorbed in the 9th Army Corps, commanded by Count d'Erlon. This general having reviewed our squadrons collected them in a circle and addressed us in terms of hearty praise. He said that he already knew our regiment, as it had served under his command during the Moreau campaign, and he trusted we would uphold in Spain the renown we had achieved under his own eyes on the farther side of the Rhine.

The six hundred men of our regiment formed four complete squadrons and were incorporated, with the same number of men and horses from the 7th and 13th Chasseurs, in General Fournier's brigade, eighteen hundred sabres strong. The 9th corps sojourned a whole month in Navarre. On September 15th we reached Salamanca by way of Burgos and Valladolid. The brigade took up its quarters in Salamanca, Toro and Zamora.

At Salamanca my position as adjutant-major secured for me elegant lodgings in the house of the beautiful Marquise Dona Rosa

de la N——, for two preceding years the widow of a Spanish colonel. Being the same as the widows of all countries, who like to keep up their pretensions, the *marquise* wished to pass for twenty-five years old—a detail which I learned from her maid. But this little fiction, if indeed it were one, was hardly needed, for whatever might have been the age of the *marquise* she was certainly one of the most attractive women I ever met. She was daintily *petite*, of a charming presence, and as airy and lively as a sylph. When she figured in a dance, with her *castanets* and tambourine, she was a Spaniard all over. When she played the piano and sang she was a genuine Italian. She had no children, and lived alone with her servants in a house of supreme luxury.

These were pleasant winter quarters; and I enjoyed them exceedingly. Every evening I spent an hour or two in the parlour with my hostess, but taking good care not to allow politics to intrude in our conversation; for the Dona Rosa, proud as all her nation, could not endure the least contradiction. Thus it came about that we eschewed all points of difference, and I had the privilege of being agreeable to the charming lady while myself enjoying a splendid good time.

On February 1st, 1812, Major de Vérigny sent for me, and ordered that at the stroke of twelve (midday) fifty *chasseurs* and an officer should mount and hold themselves in readiness, himself to assume command of the detachment. The men were to parade in light marching order, and without baggage, as they were to return on the same day. At noon the major set out with his detachment. Absolute silence had been kept concerning its mission, which proved a complete success. Here is the explanation of the whole affair.

A French merchant named Magnan, who followed the army of Prince Masséna, had sojourned for a few months at Ciudid Rodrigo on the Portuguese frontier. Desiring to return to Salamanca and to avail himself of the protection of a detachment of infantry, which was on its way to that city, he started in company with those troops, taking in the carriage a young lady, his bride of a few months. He had travelled two-thirds of the distance and was within three leagues of Salamanca, when his companion strongly urged him to hasten toward their destination. Thinking himself beyond all possible danger M. Magnan ordered his mules to be put to a brisker trot. He had barely proceeded a league farther when the carriage was arrested, in the corner of a dark wood, by a band of brigands armed to the teeth. Resistance was quite useless, and M. Magnan, his pretty young

wife, servant, mules and carriage were all hastily conducted away from the road and about half a league into the forest. The bandits, having plundered their prisoners, were about to put them to death, when the hope of obtaining a heavy ransom inspired their chief to offer M. Magnan his freedom, and that of his wife and servants, in exchange for ten thousand *francs* in gold, this sum to be paid over to an acquaintance of the bandits in Salamanca. The offer was at once accepted and M. Magnan wrote a note to one of his correspondents, ordering him to pay the bearer the amount so stipulated. At eight o'clock in the morning one of the brigands set out for Salamanca, without any visible weapons and carrying a peaceful cane. If he did not return with the gold by three in the afternoon the terrible doom of the prisoners was to be fulfilled.

Such a short and undated letter aroused the suspicion of M. Magnan's correspondent—a Frenchman who followed the army for purposes of trade. He questioned the messenger closely, but the latter, not speaking a word of French, could only rub his thumb against his forefinger, repeating as he did so the Spanish word *dinero*, which means money. The merchant concluded to send for his neighbour, Major de Vérigny, so as to acquaint him with his doubts. The major immediately had the Spaniard arrested and commanded him to tell the truth and the whole truth on up in short order. Thereupon the scoundrel

"peached," and offered to the retreat in the forest where the luckless travellers were expecting their fate. He also added that he knew of secret paths that would enable them to surprise the bandits.

"If you keep your word, and don't lead us astray," said Major de Vérigny, "I promise you both life and liberty, besides a round sum of money into the bargain."

The detachment left town at noon, as I related above. This Spaniard now rode between two *chasseurs*, who had the order to sabre him if he made the least attempt to escape. They had been pushing along for some time when the bandit cried out to them to seize on a Spaniard who was just crossing the road. He was one of the scouts of the gang, but the moment he was captured he made an offer, as the price of his freedom, to guide the detachment over a path known only to himself. The major accepted; the squad entered the forest and after a ten-minutes' gallop fell unawares upon the bandits. It was high time; for the chief was becoming distrustful and had conceded to M. Magnan a delay of but one more quarter of an hour. Before the fatal term expired Major de Vérigny and his troops dashed in and were cutting down the brigands, ere the latter had any time to grasp their blunderbusses. Several of them fell, killed or wounded, and the rest threw themselves on their knees and stretched out their hands to implore mercy from the soldiers.

The major hastened to loosen the cords with which the bandits had bound their prisoners, courteously beginning with the poor lady, who seemed more dead than alive. The travellers were put in possession of the effects that had been taken from them, and M. Magnan straightway presented five ounces to each of the two robbers who had served as guides. These the commander of the rescuing party set at liberty, urging them to live by honest ways in future. The detachment then immediately turned bridle for Salamanca, the dead, among whom was the chief, being left on the ground. The rest of the gang, nine of whom were wounded, were securely bound and huddled into two carts that were obtained by requisition for the purpose. Having been surrendered to the Spanish police, they were soon to be seen dangling from the various gibbets erected at the gates of the city. It is a method they have in Spain of dissuading the gentlemen of the highway from their special industry. This affair brought much credit to Major de Vérigny, who also, it was said, was honoured by most tender gratitude on the part of the young lady whom he had so gallantly saved from a dreadful fate. The major was but twenty-eight years old

and over five feet ten inches tall; his face was handsome, and his strikingly martial expression was enhanced by a superb moustache. He was faultless in attire and his conversation was very original and entertaining. In a word, he was an attractive man in every way.

One morning during the winter of 1811, as I happened to cross the arcade of the Salamanca public square, I met an old friend, M. V———, whom I had last seen at Augsburg in the beginning of the

campaign of 1809, when he had just graduated from the Polytechnic as a lieutenant of artillery. Now I found him wearing the uniform of an *aide-de-camp*, with a captain's epaulets and the cross of the Legion of Honour. As I manifested surprise that he should have met with so much luck, he invited me to enter the booth of Mariquita, the beautiful keeper of the coffee-house under the arcade, to enjoy a cup of chocolate while he gratified my curiosity. I gladly accepted the invita-

tion, and we were soon seated in Mariquita's, in front of two cups of rich chocolate made by her own fair hands, and some specimens of the toothsome pastry of which my friend was about as fond as he was of the pretty hostess herself.

"You were present, my dear Parquin," he said to me, "at the Wagram fight, and you certainly have not forgotten that neat action in which General Claparède was pitted against the corps of Archduke Louis, then occupying Ebersberg. During that day seven thousand French soldiers had to stand the shock of thirty-seven thousand Austrians, and withal managed to capture seven thousand prisoners, thirty guns and three hundred wagons. The emperor came up next day to review the division and to distribute the rewards. General Claparède introduced me to His Majesty as being the officer whose battery, from a position overlooking the bridge, had efficiently protected the crossing of our troops while inflicting on the enemy terrible damage. The emperor at once promoted me to a captaincy. But this was not the object of my ambition; so, keeping close in General Claparède's wake I begged him to solicit the emperor to grant me the cross. The general was kind enough to convey my request in these words:

"'Sire, here is an officer whom you have just made a captain; he is not satisfied yet, or rather, he prefers to be made a knight of the Legion of Honour.'

"The emperor turned round and looked at me with his eagle gaze.

"'Young man,' he said, 'you ask for the cross, and you are still without a beard on your face.'

"'It is true, Sire,' I answered, without losing my self-possession, 'but I needed no moustache yesterday in handling my battery.'

"The emperor was so pleased with the answer that he smiled and granted me the cross on the spot, without withdrawing my promotion as a captain. General Claparède having asked me, after the campaign, whether I should like to serve as his *aide-de-camp*, my gratitude dictated the answer, and now I am here in Spain with the division of the 9th corps commanded by General Claparède."

Captain V——— and myself were about leaving the booth of the charming Mariquita, with whom he seemed on the best of terms, when I noticed in the arcade two infantry soldiers that were holding a most animated conversation. I directed my friend's attention to them, and standing near one of the windows of the coffee-house we overheard this conversation:

"Hallo!" said one of the, soldiers to his comrade, who was rummaging in a knapsack, "is there no more swag in the camp? I thought we had still some left."

"Don't you remember," said the other fellow, "that the last piece we sold to the jeweller brought only one ounce, and we have spent every bit of it between Coimbra and this place?"

"All right, there are plenty of jewellers in Salamanca," retorted the soldier who had first spoken; "and they are not in the trade for nothing. Hold on, I think I see one here in the arcade; let us sell him a big chunk of the Saviour."

At the same time the soldier who carried the knapsack pulled out a piece of cloth, in which was a gold image of Christ six inches long, and already minus one arm.

At once the two foot-soldiers entered the jewellery store nearby to get some money for this "chunk of the Saviour"—to use their own sacrilegious expression—not much afraid, as it seemed, of the terrible consequences such an action might have for them in the world to come.

Shortly afterwards my friend and I separated. I had to wish him a pleasant journey, for he was starting next morning with his commander to join Prince Masséna's army in Portugal.

I had now been more than six months in my lodgings with the Marquise Dona Rosa de la N————, and as I had used the time to the best advantage I was really one of the most attentive cavaliers of the piquant Spaniard. At first she had declined to receive my company and

I had limited all attentions to the sending of my card. However, I soon got the maid chatting about her mistress when she came to my room with the morning chocolate, and I learned that the *marquise* watched behind a curtain of her apartment whenever I mounted my horse and -when I returned. This circumstance sufficiently emboldened me to ask her permission to enjoy daily one hour of her society. She granted my request, and thenceforth, what with lively conversation and the music of Dona Rosa I was indeed a very happy man.

It was about this time that I received, through Major de Vérigny, an order to prepare a detachment of two hundred *chasseurs*—to be taken in three equal portions from the squadrons of the 7th, 10th and 20th regiments. Two captains, two lieutenants and four second-lieutenants were to join this detachment in an expedition through the kingdom of Leon, under the orders of Major de Vérigny, whom I of course was to accompany. This first raid against the Spanish guerillas, who were daily becoming more troublesome, was to last a little more than a week. Then we were to return to Salamanca for a short time, before beginning a second expedition, which was to bring us to the city of Toro. Our third raid was to wind up at Zamora.

When I announced my departure next morning to the *marquise*, she was kind enough to bid me to supper with her. The meal was clouded by the idea of a farewell; but when I assured the *marquise*

185

that I should see her again within ten days her natural sprightliness resumed its sway. However, she declined to furnish any music that evening, although I begged her urgently to grant me this favour.

Next morning at six o'clock I was in the saddle, and on reaching the square found everybody already present. Major de Vérigny commanded, "Forward, march!" and we started in the direction of Toro. For nine days we met no guerillas. There were certainly plenty of those fellows about, but the citizens warned them of our coming, and as they had no intention to fight against desperate odds they vanished without waiting our presence. On the tenth day, however, as we were fording at a very early hour the river of La Tormès, about three leagues above Salamanca, I fell unawares upon the band commanded by El Pastor, one half of which had only just crossed the river. What remained of it on the near bank could not stand the assault of our *chasseurs*, who charged the guerillas vigorously. Several of their men were killed, others were drowned, and about a dozen were captured.

Although the victory had proved easy enough Major de Vérigny was delighted not to come back to Salamanca empty handed. Our return was in fact a veritable triumph.

The major, before we separated, gave his orders for a fresh departure on the day after the morrow, when I hastened back to my lodgings in Dona Rosa's mansion. On reaching the street door I noticed

187

that the curtains upstairs did not move, and when, later, I presented myself at the lady's parlour, the chamber-maid informed me that her mistress begged permission to remain undisturbed. I refrained from further intrusion and went to the city to meet my friends. I returned to the house rather late, and when I found myself indoors resolved to enter the *marquise's* parlour by a door off the passageway to my room. To my indignant surprise I found that it was bolted on the inside. Next morning when the maid brought in my early breakfast I despatched

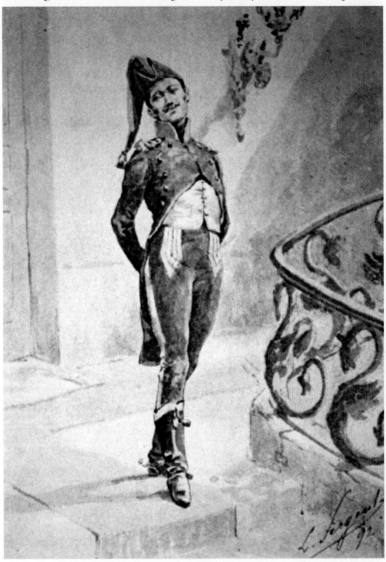

her upstairs to her mistress with a note. In answer I received an invitation to supper for the same day. I did not fail to come at the appointed time, but I remarked that during the whole meal *La Marquise* spoke of everything except the subject of my late expedition. I felt somewhat mortified but managed to restrain myself until the servants had withdrawn; then I asked her frankly in what I had offended.

"What!" she exclaimed, "do you imagine that I could ever feel friendly to one who had covered himself with the blood of my compatriots."

"My esteemed *marquise*," I answered laughing, "who would ever have thought to find you such a patriot?"

This bantering speech called forth a reply I had certainly not expected; for the *marquise* pulled out a small dagger which she always carried, and placing the point close to my heart she cried out, with such fierceness that even now the words are ringing in my ears:

"I, a patriot!—Charley, I love you; I love you a great deal too

189

much,—for every duty forbids such a love! But, if to deliver my country from the presence of these hated foreigners I had only to plunge my stiletto into your heart, you would die this very minute, and that by this very hand."

"My dear marquise," I retorted, without noticing her confession, "how much better I love to hear you with your castanets and tambourine! Please to abandon this little piece of tragedy and come back to your own self as a charming hostess."

The effect of my appeal was to bring on a violent nervous attack, and I had to call in the servants. Soon a flood of tears gave the poor lady some relief. The doctor who was hastily sent for refused to bleed her because she had just eaten supper. He had her sent to bed and gave her some soothing potion, while I could but leave the house and take a quieting walk. I returned early, however, and when the proper time came I again tried the door of the parlour. Alas, I was disappointed anew; the door was fastened! I turned "about face" and understood the situation to mean that I had received my positive dismissal.

Our detachment started next morning in the direction of Valladolid. Strange to say the enemy was constantly warned of our coming, and yet we had a fight one day with the band of l'Empecinado, which we thoroughly routed. We captured a few prisoners, whom we disposed of summarily, for we had met along the road several of our foot-soldiers hanging by the neck. It is true that the French infantry, when in Spain, indulged in a measure of recklessness that was often fatal. I remember one day to meet on the road a few soldiers who had lagged behind their battalion, and even behind the rearguard cavalry, and calling their attention to the danger they were running:

"I tell you, fellows, that if you loiter so far behind the main body of our troops you will certainly be nabbed by some of those accursed guerillas. What would you do then?"

They answered gravely: "Lieutenant, we could form a square!" There were just three of them.

One day we stopped at the village of La Neva del Rey, where we found ourselves very comfortably situated, the supplies being abundant and the inn fairly good. They gave us for waiter a kind of Don Figaro, who was so bright and entertaining that Major de Vérigny took a liking to him, and invited him to drink spiced wine at the supper-table while we were smoking our cigarettes. He played the tambourine splendidly, danced with gracefulness, and sang his Spanish songs in a most pleasing voice. We imagined the fellow to be a son or nephew of the innkeeper. He remained with us until midnight, when he vanished; we supposed he had gone to bed. Having to start at dawn of day we ourselves spent the rest of the night around the table, drinking spiced wine.

Next morning at five o'clock, just after I quitted the village, I was surprised to notice an old ragged shepherd who, from the midst of his flock, beckoned me to approach. I left the head of the detachment and rode over toward the man. From under his blouse he pulled a letter which he gave me. Judge of my surprise when I found written in French:

"To the Adjutant-Major of the detachment, to be handed by him to Major de Vérigny, in command of the Contra-Guerillas of the French Army."

Assuming that this letter had something to do with the service, I opened it. It read as follows:

"Commander! I El Pastor, with whose hand you have had a scuffle near the La Tormès fording place, have always desired to meet you personally, as I was greatly moved by your generosity in sparing the lives of several of my men, who have since escaped the prisons of Salamanca and joined me. I therefore disguised myself, and having the fullest confidence in the innkeeper of La Neva del Rey, I introduced myself to you, and thus became fully informed: First—Of the manner in which you guard your person. Second—of the kind of life you lead. Concerning the first of these points allow me to congratulate you. You keep a pretty close watch around your quarters—otherwise you may depend that the 'waiter' who served you so attentively at the inn last evening, would have dropped upon you unawares with his troop in the middle of the night. As for how you live and pass your time—I must also compliment you heartily. Indeed you know as well how to enjoy life as you know how to fight. It is so unpleasant for me to fight against men for whom I feel the esteem you have inspired, that I have decided to leave this province and go seek for other adversaries. I wish you good health and good luck."

I continued my way after having given the shepherd a silver piece, and hastened to place the letter in Major de Vérigny's hands, stating that I had opened it believing it to concern my duties. The major approved and advised me not to mention the letter to anyone, as otherwise General Fournier, who commanded at Salamanca, would certainly exact a large money penalty from the innkeeper of La Neva del Rey, for his share in this little practical joke.

We made our second halt at Valladolid and on the following day set out for the third campaign. Toward the middle of that day, as I rode at the head of my detachment, I could easily see over the walls of a house that had recently been gutted by fire. I was surprised to notice within some object that glittered with extraordinary brilliancy in the rays of the sun. I gave my trumpeter the order to investigate when he called back to me at once in an excited manner:

"Adjutant-Major, there are a couple of the brigands' horses here, saddled and ready for fight!"

I immediately detached twenty-five men to surround the ruins and to search them in every corner. They found the two horses seen by the trumpeter, which were hitched to a post and munching at a feed of barley spilled out on a cloak. The pistols that were in the saddle holsters proved to be of French make. It was their metallic mountings that had reflected the rays of the sun and thus revealed the presence of the two steeds. Lances were also suspended from the bow of each saddle. The riders were certainly not very far off and yet we caught no glimpse of human beings. Suddenly I was struck with an idea that by ascending to the top of a neighbouring hillock, which overlooked the plain, I might discover the horsemen. It turned out as I thought, for we at once espied two guerillas running across the fields toward the forest. When the cavalrymen I sent after them were almost upon the fugitives the latter stopped, breathless, and were captured. I brought them to Major de Vérigny, who closely questioned them. They declared that they belonged to a guerilla force commanded by a friar. This ex-monk was maintaining a blockade on the road between Valladolid and Salamanca. His custom was to hang his prisoners to improvised gallows planted along the road, and even in some cases to disfigure the bodies of his unfortunate victims.

In spite of this brutal conduct on the part of their chief, Major de Vérigny resolved to bring the bandits captive as far as Zamora, and doubtless the fellows might have had their lives spared if the major had not ordered me to search their pockets. One of the guerillas, who seemed to be something of a leader, and who bore upon his face the half-healed scar from a recent sabre-cut, was found in possession of a pocketbook, in which was a receipt on blue paper written in French by our military postmaster at Valladolid. It was the pocketbook of a French officer whose corpse we had found stretched upon the road. You may imagine that this discovery settled the fate of the rascals. Major de Vérigny made them kneel down against the wall of the house wherein the horses had been captured. A squad of men levelled their guns and—the two bandits fell shot through the heart while devoutly making the sign of the cross.

The day before we reached Zamora an officer and twenty-five *chasseurs* from the 7th Regiment joined us. The officer brought us an order to wheel towards the left as far as a certain ferry on the Douro River. We were to reach it before daybreak, so as to swoop upon a hand of smugglers who proposed to use the ferry boat for transferring to the other side a lot of contraband wares, especially imported groceries. We fulfilled our orders as they were given to us.

The place had been so accurately indicated, and every precaution was so shrewdly taken that nothing escaped us; neither men nor goods. Everything was brought over to Zamora with the exception of a few quick-witted muleteers, who contrived to escape by the way. Major de Vérigny took advantage of the circumstance to distribute their mules among the officers of his detachment. It was the only reward we gathered from a whole month's campaigning.

On May 1st, 1811, the Fournier brigade left its cantonments and we advanced to Ciudad-Rodrigo, where we were incorporated in the division of General Montbrun. He was one of the finest commanders I ever met in my life. Already he was famous throughout the army for his extraordinary bravery, and for the quaint reply he had made one

day while bivouacking at Zuaim, during the campaign of 1809. Captain Lindsay, his *aide-de-camp*, had rushed toward him at full gallop and when he came within hearing distance, cried out:

" Good news. General, good news! I have just come in from Vienna and I am delighted to tell you that peace is concluded!"

"What the deuce is that to me, sir, whose only trade is in whacks and slashes," was the general's indignant answer.

Though not above thirty years old he was already a lieutenant-general, a Count of the Empire, with one hundred thousand *francs* income and a well-won military reputation. He was also the husband of a young and charming wife, and yet he seemed to enjoy himself only upon the battlefield and to prefer a thousand times the life of a bivouac to all the so-called pleasures of society. His ardent longing to die a soldier's death was granted him all too soon, for at the Battle of the Moskowa he was killed by a cannonball striking him full in the breast.

We had just joined our forces with those of the army of Portugal. It was on the 3rd of May, while reconnoitring about three leagues from Ciudad-Rodrigo, that we saw for the first time the English army. Major de Vérigny, who was in charge of the line of skirmishers from our brigade, being very desirous to make the acquaintance of the English officers, said to me

"Parquin, here is a bottle of capital French brandy. Set off with it on a gallop toward the English line, wave your white handkerchief, and when they approach to ask what is the matter, say that you have come to invite them to touch glasses with the officers they will soon have to fight. If they accept the courtesy my officers and I will join you at once."

The major had hardly finished when I started at full gallop, having the brandy bottle in my sabretache and a white handkerchief in my right hand. The latter I waved up and down as soon as I was at a reasonable distance from the English lines. An officer of the 10th English Dragoons galloped toward me at once, asking what was my errand.

"I have here a bottle of brandy, sir, which my comrades and myself offer to drink with you and your friends before we meet for another purpose."

The English officer accepted and signalled to his comrades to advance; I did the same to Major de Vérigny, who joined me with about ten of our fellows just as the same number of English officers were coming to the rendezvous. The bottle went the rounds and was emptied quickly enough. The brandy was pronounced excellent, especially by the English officers who seemed quite pleased by our civility. A general conversation

was entered into; they first asked us how long we had been in Spain.

"We have been here but a short time," I answered them; "two years ago we were fighting the Austrians and now we come hither from France, gentlemen, to make *your* acquaintance."

"You are welcome," they responded, all together. One of them

added with some pride: "Oh, we already know the Élite cavalry of the French Army; we have had dealings with the regiments of the Guides of Napoleon, for we captured their chief, General Lefébvre-Desnouettes, at Benavente."

Major de Vérigny promptly answered:

"Ah, yes, it was a rash move of that commander to attack twenty of your squadrons with but four squadrons of his Guides; and this along with a false direction. which prevented him from striking the river ford, sufficiently explains his defeat. Never mind, gentlemen, we shall probably have a chance during the coming campaign to avenge the mishap to the Guides."

An English officer inquired if any among us were acquainted in the French city of Moulins, as he desired a letter to be transmitted to one of his compatriots just then a prisoner in that city. Adjutant-Major Dulimbert of the 10th Chasseurs, whose father was then prefect of Moulins, accepted the commission and on the following day the letter was handed him under cover of a flag of truce.

It appeared that this conversation was rather longer than the English general relished, for two or three shells fired by the English artillery fell but a short distance from the group and compelled us to take our leave; not however before sampling some fine British rum, which the English officers insisted we should accept at their hands.

We operated our retreat toward Ciudad-Rodrigo in echelon formation, for this was only a reconnoitring expedition in the direction of the enemy. Half an hour after our interview with the English officers we heard a few carbine shots and loud shouts, and saw a squad of skirmishers to our right, vigorously pursued by the enemy, while Lieutenant Fage of the 13th Chasseurs was beckoning us with his sabre to come over to his assistance. Without stopping the march of the column I started on a gallop, calling after me a number of officers and non-commissioned officers. Our party soon grew to about fifty troopers and we charged toward the right to give help to the skirmishers' squad. We dashed furiously against the English, who were compelled to leave behind a few of our men whom they had already made prisoners, and we even captured several of the light dragoons. During this movement I was highly pleased with the conduct of Adjutant Doberseux, whose promotion I had effected shortly after my arrival in Spain. But we were soon in our turn charged by the English cavalry.

I remember that when we re-entered our line, away from which we had wandered quite a distance, I noticed on the road one of our comrades in a critical situation. He was an officer of my own regiment, named Jouglas. His horse, which he had dubbed "Madcap," because of the fury it took on in a charge, had suddenly balked in the way and refused to answer either bridle or spurs.

"What the deuce are you doing here, Jouglas?" I queried.

"My horse has just balked," he replied, "and he won't budge from the spot. I guess he is played out."

"Then you may expect to be cut down by the English, for they are after us like a hurricane."

On hearing this Jouglas struck the side of his horse's head with the flat of his sword, on which the animal at last obeyed him and flew off toward the left with the wild rush that had earned it the surname of "Madcap."

We reached the bivouac rather late in the evening, with our captured dragoons. Next morning General Fournier sent for me from Ciudad-Rodrigo, where he had his headquarters, and assured me to the command of a detachment consisting of a trumpeter, fifty *chasseurs*, a lieutenant and a second lieutenant. I was ordered to reconnoitre a, Spanish village which was pointed out to me upon the map, its location being about two leagues from Almeida, on the Portuguese frontier. There I was to gather all possible information touching the movements of the English.

199

On the stroke of ten o'clock I entered the village. It was rather a large place and I traversed it at full gallop. I posted my sentries some distance on the farther side, and ordered half of the men to dismount, unbridle their horses, and give them fodder and drink. This service completed the other half were to do likewise. The men were supplied with provisions by the local authorities.

As I entered the village I caught a Spanish drummer reading a proclamation aloud to the inhabitants, requesting them to come to the assistance of Don Julian's guerillas, so as to enable him to recuperate the losses that he had recently suffered in men and horses. "It is," ran the proclamation, "the last appeal the *alcalde* (or mayor) of this village will make in his behalf, and after this day and date no further subscriptions will be accepted."

As soon as I had the troop in position, I rode with my trumpeter over to the *alcalde's* office, and was there told that on the preceding

night a strong English patrol had ridden through the village on a
tour of reconnaissance along the Almeida road, but that they had
not levied anything from the citizens. On this information being
given by the old gentleman I pulled out of my sabretache the proclamation I had just confiscated from the village drummer, and commanded the *alcalde* to hand over at once the money he had collected
for Don Julian's guerillas. The poor man, who thought he would be
hanged for his share in the business, was only too glad to conduct

me into his library and there fish out from behind his bookcase a box containing over six thousand *francs* in gold, silver and small change. I divided the amount into two parts: One of three thousand *francs* for my *chasseurs*, and the other, also of three thousand *francs*, fifteen hundred *francs* in gold for myself, and fifteen hundred *francs* for the two officers associated with me in the command. I thus distributed the money, only requiring from all concerned a pledge of absolute secrecy. We then returned to Ciudad-Rodrigo and I presented a report of my expedition.

Next morning our brigade mounted horse. General Fournier and the 13th Chasseurs spent the day and the following night in the village I had visited the day before. I was then with my regiment bivouacking about one league beyond, and I had hardly settled down for the night's rest, when an orderly reached me with a pressing order from General Fournier. He was quartered at the house of the *alcalde*, and had hardly entered it when he made a demand for money

"You come too late, general," replied the old man; "an officer who visited us yesterday morning has taken with him the only six thousand *francs* I had in my possession."

Of course the matter was clear enough; the officer who had reconnoitred the village was none other than myself, and that was the reason why the general sent for me. He received me with much temper and ordered that I should hand him over at once the six thousand *francs* I had collected.

"I am sorry to say, general," I answered him with perfect composure, "that I have at your command only one-fourth the amount you name; the other three-fourths have been distributed to the detachment and its officers. Meanwhile kindly allow me, general, to mention to you the fact that for more than a year I have not received one *franc* of pay, and that the government has not given me the wherewithal to keep three good horses, to supply myself with proper maps of the regions we traverse, and to be ever ready to march when a difficult expedition is on hand. Don't you think, general, that it is only fair I should make the best of any chance that might offer itself to replenish my purse, depleted by this long delay in the payment of services."

I was pulling out of my belt the fifteen hundred *francs* when the general stopped me with a very amiable gesture.

"The loyal fashion in which you have distributed the six thousand *francs* among your troops impels me to pass over this matter. But don't let such a thing happen again without notifying me beforehand."

205

I thanked General Fournier—who indeed might well be indulgent concerning all such forced levies—and went back to my regiment.

I noticed next day, the 5th of May, as I was mounting quite early, that Major de Vérigny was neatly shaved and wearing a fresh pair of gloves, while his boots shone like a mirror and his spurs were almost dazzling. Moreover, he was riding his fine Arabian mare, his war steed, whose trappings were covered with braid and spangles. His colback also was decked with its plume and the streamer flew wide and free; his moustache was curled and waxed—in a word, he was in true gala uniform and I could not do less than complement him on his spruce appearance

"My dear Parquin," he said to me, "that is the way we should all dress when about to face the enemy. One can never be too grandly arrayed when the ball is to open with cannon fire."

The brigade having been mustered we rode on our way and after two hour's' march joined the cavalry division of General Montbrun, taking up a battle position to the right. The English army was in line on the Portuguese frontier, and in a very formidable position, having a river behind it and flanked by two defiles rendered impassable by the swollen mountain torrents. Our army, which bore the name of the Army of Portugal, was commanded by Prince Masséna, and had lately been increased by General Fournier's brigade, General Claparède's infantry division, and fifteen hundred men from the Imperial Guard cavalry sent over by Marshal Bessières from Valladolid to take part in the fighting. Our forces would have been about equal in number to those of the English Army had it not been for the crowds of Portuguese and Spanish insurgents that hung on to the enemy. All our men were full of fight and only too anxious to come to close quarters with the English.

But neither the gallant conduct of the Claparède division on the right of the battlefield, nor the vigorous charge of the four Élite companies of the 6th, 11th, 15th and 25th dragoons, led with so much bravery through the English lines by Colonel Ornano, nor any other influence, indeed, could persuade Prince Masséna to leave his camp, where he had closeted himself with General Loison. The day before he had been notified from France that he would be replaced in his command by the Marshal Duke of Ragusa, who was daily expected at headquarters. Accordingly this battle, which throughout the entire morning had turned to our advantage, was terminated suddenly just as the English general was beginning his retreat.

The Fournier brigade was the last corps that engaged the enemy. It was while charging a body of English cavalry, which he completely

routed, that General Fournier had his horse shot under him. The chief-
major of the regiment and Captain Lasalle, Lieutenant Labassée, Lieutenant Himonet, and a number of *chasseurs* were unhorsed and disabled
by the artillery and infantry of the enemy, and I myself received a
short-range bullet which tore through my face and broke six teeth.

One of the peculiar gifts of Major de Vérigny was the style in which
he could speak to his soldiers so as to electrify them in critical moments.

During the morning of May the 5th, as I have just narrated, our squadron had been for some time under the direct fire of the enemy's artillery. Major de Vérigny and myself were riding through the ranks at a walking pace, while the major addressed one or another of the soldiers, as was his constant habit in a time of danger.

"Parquin," he suddenly said to me, pointing his finger at a *chasseur* who was in battle for the first time and who showed trepidation in his pallid face, "I can see by this fellow's countenance that the moment we begin charging he will use his sabre like a hero."

The soldier's courage was marvellously revived by these words, and he at once brandished his sabre, exclaiming: "You are just right, I will, Major." The man kept his word, for a few moments later he was among the first to pierce the English lines, where he met his doom.

Major de Vérigny, hearing that I had been wounded, was kind enough to send an inquiry about me. I wrote with a pencil the following note, which I sent back to him by his orderly:

"My wound does not amount to anything: I had a keen tooth for the English and they were anxious to pull it out, but they have been so mean as to knock out six more at the same time."

Marshal the Duke of Ragusa arrived on the 12th of May and met with a hearty welcome. He speedily reorganized the army of Portugal. In the meantime my wound was getting better every day though for

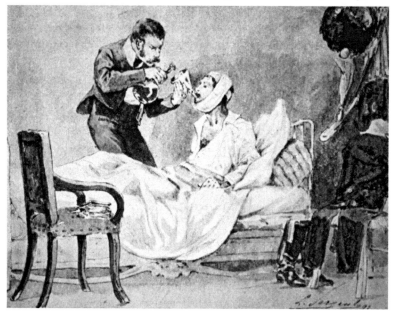

a week I could take no other nourishment than some *bouillon*, which an orderly poured into my mouth by means of a funnel. After the first few days my wound did not cause much pain, but it compelled me to remain perfectly silent. I was not long in getting well, however, for it is a known fact that face-wounds heal more readily than any other.

We were now quartered in the vicinity of Salamanca. I was hardly recovered when General Fournier was informed that Don Julian was planning to visit the Zamora road, and he ordered me to proceed with fifty *chasseurs* and strike the guerilla chief effectively. I surprised the insurgents and their commander in a village where they had taken up quarters for the night. I captured many of them but failed to make Don Julian himself a prisoner, this resolute fellow having sprung on a bare-backed horse and made his escape, leaving behind his papers and considerable baggage. The *chasseurs* of the 20th this time gathered in a quantity of valuable booty. General Fournier congratulated me on the outcome of my brief expedition. It was doubtless on account of it that he commissioned me a few days

later to be the bearer of an important despatch to General Kellermann, at Valladolid The general authorized me to take an escort of twenty-five men; but I urged on him the fact that I had only to ride a distance of fifteen leagues, and that by starting at break of day, with only one orderly, I could accomplish my mission without hindrance and with much greater despatch.

The general agreeing to this I set out at the time appointed and along about eleven o'clock reached a lonely inn about half way between Salamanca and Valladolid. There I expected to get a relay of fresh horses to enable me to continue my route at full speed. How great was my amazement on entering the courtyard to find it filled with men, horses and mules, all comfortably bivouacking. I had fallen upon a band of guerrillas commanded by the Lieutenant D'Aguilar.

Any resistance was of course useless; all I could do was to maintain a firm and resolute countenance. Having been led, disarmed, before the guerilla chieftain, I said to him:

"My life is in your hands; it is by my own imprudence you have this advantage. Be thankful, however, for my rashness, for if I had taken along an escort you would now be in my power instead of I in yours. Be careful, however, what you do; for if a single hair of our heads should fall, tomorrow ten of your comrades who are captive at Salamanca will be done to death."

Having spoken in those terms I took with the utmost friendliness a cigarette which Lieutenant D'Aguilar held in his mouth, knowing this to be a high compliment to a Spaniard. I quietly began smoking it and sat down without betraying any concern to await the sentence that should be passed upon us.

A deep silence reigned throughout the numerous assembly, so boisterous but a few minutes before. The chief began interpreting my words to his men. After some moments he turned and said to me:

"See here, hell-hound; you need not imagine our decision to be affected by the thought of what may happen to our captured friends—like all good Spaniards they would know how to die for God and their country. Merely to kill you, however, would not rid our country of those that oppress it. Your life is safe; here are your weapons, and let us

be friends for a little space. You are freely welcome to the hospitality of a guerilla chief."

As he finished speaking he stretched forth his hand, which I pressed with unfeigned gratitude. My orderly, who had proven to be coolness itself, took his share of the frugal meal that was offered us, after which we mounted our horses and left. We continued on the road to Valladolid, which we reached at dawn of day. I must acknowledge that since this event, and during the whole year I sojourned in Spain, I took every opportunity to be of service to the Spaniards who fell into our hands and I believe that on several occasions I merited their warmest gratitude.

When I returned to my regiment and narrated this adventure Major de Vérigny said to me:

"Parquin, you have lately had two very narrow escapes: the first

time the English were after you and now you have come pretty close to an improvised gallows."

"Well," I answered him smiling, "I think I am rather hard to kill, and I honestly believe that if I am killed I shall come to life again. Such things have been told of others, haven't they?"

During the early days of June the Marshal Duke of Ragusa moved

his army toward Badajoz, which was then besieged by the enemy. We arrived there just in time to deliver the city. The forts—that of St. Nicholas, especially—had already been stormed twice. A few English who were surprised by the dawning day as well as by the advent of our troops, just as they were scaling the walls, clambered up their own ladders into the fort and surrendered unconditionally rather than stand the fire of our infantry, which had opened a fusillade on them. General Wellington did not care to meet the united armies of Marshal Soult and the Duke of Ragusa, which had joined forces at Mérida. We pursued his army as far as the outskirts of the fortified city of Campo-Mayor, in Portugal. Marshal Soult settled down in Seville and the army of Portugal was quartered in and around Mérida, the staff being lodged in the city and the Montbrun division at Médellin. It was while we sojourned there that the first-major, then in command of our regiment, informed me that the marshal had asked to have attached to his general staff a cavalry officer provided with a good mount and a keen active brain. The major at once thought of me. I gratefully accepted the position and went over to Mérida next day. I was far from anticipating the unpleasant experience that awaited me at headquarters.

I had been in Mérida but a couple of days when I received a letter from an officer of my own regiment named Duclos, begging me to cash for him a credit-note of two hundred and fifty-nine *francs*. The vouchers for the use to which this money had been but were joined to the letter. I went over with these documents to the paymaster-general of the army, whose post, in his absence, was filled by his brother, a division paymaster.

When I reached the paymaster-general's office, about noon, one of the clerks said to me; "The paymaster is taking his midday nap; you cannot see him." I returned at six o'clock, and they answered me: "The paymaster is at dinner." Rather chafed by this curt answer I said in a loud voice: "*Parbleu!* If the paymaster spends all his time gadding about how shall I ever find him? Is there any one here that takes his place?"

The paymaster, who had overheard me, at once sallied out of the dining-room, napkin in hand, and going over to his desk examined my vouchers with a scowl on his face. He asked me whether I was the M. Duclos designated in the papers. I said I was not, but instantly submitted to him the note from my friend which authorized me to cash the credit for his account. The paymaster dismissed me quite brusquely saying that he declined to recognize the transfer. I was going down the stairs in high dudgeon when a polite clerk ran after me and advised me to call on M. Marchand, quartermaster-general of the army, assuring me that he would make things right the moment he had examined my papers. Straight I went to the quartermaster-general's house and found him also at dinner; but he came out as soon as he heard that an officer was asking for him. He looked over my documents and kindly wrote across M. Duclos' note: "Payable to M. Parquin, officer in the same regiment, who is authorized to cash this note for M. Duclos' account." It was too late to return to the paymaster's office but I went there first thing in the morning. the functionary, whose name was M. Malet, this time happened to be at his desk, but after perusing the quartermaster-general's indorsement he returned the paper to me, saying:

"M. Marchand does not know what he is about: neither do you. I shall not pay this credit."

"I see that your mind is made up, sir," I retorted; "but I was cer-

tainly entitled to a more polite reception; I hope, therefore, that you will accord the usual satisfaction for having treated me so flippantly."

"The rank I hold in the army," answered M. Malet, with a great show of indifference, " places me much higher than a subaltern in your grade. Leave my office, sir, or I will have you put out by my orderly."

I left at once, but not without saying; "Be assured, Mr. Paymaster, that I shall remember your behaviour in this matter."

When I returned to my quarters I found awaiting me an order from the chief of the general staff of the army, to take charge of a detachment of fifty men of the 7th Infantry, commanded by an officer, and start with them for Almaraz-on-the-Tagus, there to make sure whether the bridge which the marshal had ordered thrown over the river was adequately constructed. This expedition lasted a whole week without our meeting any mishap; but, as I was approaching the city of Truxillo on my return, in the midst of a very arid plain, with no village in sight, we suddenly perceived a cloud of dust rising in the distance. The infantry officer, who was accustomed to guerilla surprises, said to me:

"Do you notice my dear comrade that cloud of dust on our right? In five minutes time we shall be having a lively brush with the Spaniards."

We had bayonets affixed to the guns, which were loaded, and so continued on our march. The infantry officer's surmise proved true to the letter; the guerillas were very soon upon us, howling like demons; but in the nick of time the officer commanded: "Halt! Present—Fire!" Next minute the Spaniards had turned about face like a flock of pigeons, although not without having sent into our ranks a hail of bullets, one of which struck the infantry officer in the thigh. I at once jumped from my horse, put the officer in my saddle, and took sole command of the detachment. During the few minutes that were needed to bandage the officer's leg with my handkerchief I had to halt the detachment, but I took the precaution to command: "Bayonets—ready!"

Noticing this pause in our advance, the guerillas returned toward us, and one of them shouted to the escort.

"Soldiers! Give up that cavalry officer who bears the despatches; we don't want to hurt you, for we are your friends."

These words having been spoken in French made me think that the fellows must have among them a deserter. Of course the soldiers did not yield for a moment to the infamous proposal, and when the guerillas were but ten feet away I ordered a, fusillade which again scattered them. Several of the Spaniards fell grievously wounded; one of them, whose horse had been killed, was captured. As I was about to have him shot on the instant, I bethought myself of telling the officer of the escort and his soldiers how I had lately owed my life to the generosity of a guerilla chief, a lieutenant D'Aguilar. I concluded by begging the officer to permit me to have my preference concerning the prisoner.

"My dear comrade," he answered, "this fellow is your prisoner rather than mine, so do with him what you please; for although the guerillas have wounded me I infer that they were especially seeking after you."

"I thank you heartily," I said, pressing his hand, "and since your soldiers have also heard my story, let me ask them if they indorse the permission you have given me."

From all sides the men cried out: "Yes, yes, do with this man what you please." I then wrote on a scrap of paper the following declaration:

"Charles Parquin, an officer of the 20th Chasseurs, having been made prisoner by the Lieutenant D'Aguilar and his guerillas a short distance from Salamanca, and owing his life and that of his orderly to their generosity, takes this occasion to give proof of his gratitude by according both life and liberty on this 10th day of January, 1811, to a Spaniard of the guerilla band of El Medico."

I handed this paper to the Spaniard, who told me he could read it. I added one gold ounce and gave the man his liberty, with a cordially expressed wish never to meet him again on our road. The poor fellow, who had been all this time more dead than alive, embraced my knees while making the sign of the cross and soon vanished.

When we arrived at Truxillo we met an infantry battalion which had started to our assistance, for the smoke of the fusillade had been noticed from the top of the city walls. The officer in command of my detachment remained at Truxillo to have his wound attended to, while I took charge of the escort as far as Mérida.

Having rendered a full account of the incident to the chief of staff, I hurried to my lodgings to put on a fresh uniform and call upon the proprietor of the house I dwelt in, who happened to be a very handsome and charming woman. My orderly informed me, to my decided chagrin, that since my departure Paymaster Malet had become a frequent visitor at the house, and that he was wont every evening to come over and spend a couple of hours with the lady proprietor. In fact he was at that moment paying her a visit.

"Ha, ha!" I said to myself, "here is a most excellent chance to get even with the insolent jackanapes."

As soon I was dressed I strode up to the next floor and walked into my hostess' presence, at once taking permission to kiss her shapely hand. The paymaster, who stood by her chair, hat in hand, was about withdrawing. I feared that the satisfaction I craved for was almost escaping me, so I turned toward him brusquely.

"Mister Paymaster," I said, "how does it happen that you, who are so ill-mannered in your own lodgings, dare to visit other people's?"

"You will please to notice, sir, that I am not in your lodgings, but in *Madame's* apartment."

"That may be, but it does not deprive me of the right of saying straight out, and wherever I meet you, that you are nothing but an impertinent cad."

Not waiting for any more the paymaster left the room, but I followed him into the passage and called out to my orderly, who was standing downstairs: "Turn out that individual—I have forbidden him ever to enter this house again." The paymaster, who was a strongly-built man, attempted some resistance, but my men speedily threw him out.

My object, of course, was to compel him to fight with me. I felt so sure that he would go directly to the chief of the general staff, to complain against me, that I was not long in presenting myself at that officer's quarters, where my enemy was telling his story with violent emphasis.

"But what are you complaining of," I interposed. "Did you not rudely dismiss me only a week ago from your presence? Today I simply return the courtesy. There is this difference, however, between you and me: you refused then to grant me satisfaction, while I have come here today, sir, to place myself at your disposal."

"Enough, sir," retorted M. Malet, "you won't have long to wait before receiving a message from me."

And just an hour later I was in receipt of the following note:

"Sir: The conduct you have been guilty of toward me is unworthy of an officer and deserves condign punishment. Accordingly I shall await you tomorrow at five o'clock in the morning on the farther side of the bridge, and shall there administer to you the chastisement you merit at my sword's point.

"Malet.

"Division Paymaster, Acting Paymaster-General of the Army of Portugal."

I acknowledged the receipt of this letter and went to bed. Exactly at four o'clock next morning I left my quarters and walked into the city square. There I met a captain of grenadiers of the 70th Infantry, called Bellegarde, and also nicknamed "Branch of Gold," whom I knew to be chief fencing-master of the 70th.

"Will you be kind enough, captain," I asked him, "to lend me your sword, with another sword exactly like it, if you should chance to possess it. Here is the reason why I need the weapons." And I showed him the paymaster's letter.

"My swords are quite at your disposal, comrade," answered the captain, "on one condition, however; and that is, that I shall accompany them to the rendezvous."

"That is all right," I exclaimed, " I shall be only too happy to have you as my second." And we started at once for the meeting place. On arriving we found the paymaster already there, dressed in an embroidered coat, a pair of duck trousers, and riding boots. I was clad in my swallow-tail uniform, with nankeen trousers and low shoes. Two minutes later the paymaster chose one of the swords and threw his coat aside. He then said to me, with an air of impertinence:

" You are rather slow getting ready, sir!"

I had used a little longer time than he, for I had taken off my vest and undervest.

"You won't lose anything by waiting awhile," I retorted, falling into guard.

I quickly realized that I had to deal with a very expert swordsman, but having extricated my weapon by an adroit movement of the wrist, I thrust the blade beneath his and touched his right suspender, the buckle of which stopped the sword. However, the blood spurted.

"You are wounded, paymaster," said my second.

"Oh, that is nothing," he answered with perfect composure.

Again we crossed swords, but this little mishap had rendered him much more cautious and he ceased to lead the fight. It was then my turn to advance briskly, and by a succession of rapid changes of front, followed up with cut and thrust, I forced him backward into a piece of ground that had lately been tilled. There he found his big riding boots very much of an incumbrance. To make the story short, I followed up a lightning pass by a swift lunge, bringing my sword into direct contact with his right side, which it penetrated, when the man fell. I rushed toward him with extended hands but my second, Captain Bellegarde, called out:

"I say, paymaster, before you pass over finally it were best to hand us the key to your safe."

"Instead of coining poor jokes," I said rather sharply to Captain Bellegarde, "you had better help me do something for my brave adversary."

The paymaster's seconds, who had hurriedly started in search of help, soon returned with two privates who rapidly improvised a stretcher and bore the wounded man to his quarters. A surgeon-major was sent for, who dressed the wound and ordered silence to be kept around his patient, giving us the best hopes, however, that his injury would not have any fatal consequences. Our *cortège* was met by General Ferey, who was just then taking a morning ride with his

aide-de-camp. Of course these gentlemen reported the matter speedily to headquarters.

I had hardly re-entered my rooms before an orderly of Marshal
Marmont came in with the word to report myself. I donned my uniform and obeyed the command at once. The moment I reached the
marshal's presence he said to me:

"So it is you, sir, only just attached to my staff, who begin by
thrusting your sword through my paymaster-general?"

My answer was to pull out of my sabretache the paymaster's letter,
which I had taken care to bring along with me, and hand it to the
duke, explaining:

"My lord, here is my justification. I humbly beg you to read it through."
The marshal perused the letter, and then returned it to me, saying:

"The paymaster has only got what he deserves. I now remember that when he was under my orders in Illyria he successively wounded two infantry officers with whom he had set up a quarrel."

Thereupon the marshal dismissed me without further parley.

A short time after my duel, having learned that Mr. Paymaster gave two hours daily to a *siesta*, I again went over to his office and presented for payment the draft of my friend Duclos. This time the clerk hastened into the paymaster's room to inquire if he should honour the demand, when I distinctly heard my rival say to him: "Yes, yes! pay the gentlemen in gold."

Three ounces of gold were accordingly handed over to me, being in full settlement of the note for two hundred and forty *francs* which had caused me so many vexations.

On the 20th of August Major de Vérigny arrived at headquarters from Médellin, whence he had been summoned by the marshal, who knew him well, to take command of the latter's personal escort. This escort was composed in the following manner. Not to deprive any two regiments of their Élite companies, which would have greatly impaired the efficiency of such organizations, the marshal had requisitioned one officer and twenty-five men from the Élite company of each of his eight cavalry regiments, thus creating an escort of two hundred men with their officers. Of this picked body the major proudly assumed command and entreated the duke to give me to him for adjutant-major. His request on this point was cheerfully granted, which was all the pleasanter to myself as it showed the marshal in command to have no hard feeling against me for the little lesson I taught his paymaster.

It will be remembered that about the middle of June, by the aid of Marshal Soult and his army, we had relieved Badajoz from investment and pushed the British forces in the direction of Portugal. In September, three months afterward, we were again confronting the English Army, which was now laying siege to Ciudad-Rodrigo. Ten thousand men from our army of the North, the whole Imperial Guard, under the brave and handsome General Dorsenne, here joined the division under the Marshal Duke of Ragusa. On this it was deemed prudent by the English commander not to tarry for the arrival of our troops, and he once more effected a retreat into Portugal, pursuant to his plan of constant procrastination, which though not very heroic, was after all most disastrous to our interests. We followed his army for some time, and one day even missed a chance to strike for good and all this formidable adversary. We had been informed by a deserter that General Wellington was just then in the midst of a hollow square of troops of his rearguard, in company with the Prince of Orange, who acted as his *aide-de-camp*. We neglected to capture this square—a task comparatively easy at the time. The information had come too late.

Our brigade did not relinquish the habit of drinking a few glasses of rum and brandy with the English officers whenever we were thrown out as skirmishers in front of their line. Our *chasseurs* had a ruder way of procuring rum when they felt like drinking it; occasionally you would hear one brave fellow exclaim to another:

"Say, we have no more brandy; who is going to nip that Goddam's flask?" (This word was the usual nickname given to the English soldiers). Then a *chasseur* would be drawn by lot to capture the first Englishman he could lay hands upon and secure his rum-bottle. If successful the *chasseur* was entitled to a bounty of three *napoleons*, which was the regular sum paid for every horse of the enemy thus secured.

The English officers are very courageous and very good company, but sometimes they are also very sarcastic. We were informed at the recapture of the city of Abrantès, in Portugal, that these gentlemen felt like apologizing most humbly because this circumstance had prevented the Duchess of Abrantès from giving birth to her child in the capital of her duchy, for which special purpose she had come all the way from Paris into Spain.

"Indeed the Duchess of Abrantès," said the English officers, "must think we are scarcely entitled to the name of gentlemen;" and they begged us to ask her to excuse them.

They also tried to play jokes upon us. During the retreat into Portugal, near the city of Sabugal, one of the officers of our brigade, M. Fage of the 13th Chasseurs, undertook to pursue an English officer, who, mounted on an excellent horse, just managed to keep ten feet ahead of the Frenchman, not allowing him at any moment to shorten the distance.

From time to time the Englishman would turn in his saddle, without slacking speed, and address his pursuer in a tone of polite irony:

"I am sure you are riding a Norman horse, sir."

Somewhat vexed by the repeated banter, Fage pulled out his pistol and fired at the Briton, but the hammer only flashed in the pan.

"I understand," remarked the Englishman, without twitching a muscle, "your pistol must be of that clumsy manufacture of Versailles!"

Made furious by this new raillery Fage cried out:

"Then wait for me a minute, and we shall try which of our sabres is the keener and better handled!"

But the English officer declined the proposal, for we were known to be quite agile in the use of our swords—this of course being a reflection on English bravery. It was our practice to use the point of our sabres, while the Englishmen always struck with the blade, which was three inches in width. Thus it happened that out of twenty of their blows nineteen miscarried; but of course if the edge reached you the result was extremely painful.

Nor was it at all rare to see an arm cut clean off the body. This very

thing, indeed, is what happened to brave Colonel Sourd of the 2nd Lancers, who lost his arm at Waterloo.

Under the walls of the city of Sabugal we of the marshal's escort witnessed a magnificent dragoon charge, led by General Carrié, who was wounded and made prisoner in it, his horse having stumbled down in ten midst of the English lines. It was easy to see from a dis-

tance what losses the Hanoverian light horse suffered from our dragoons, as almost every thrust of our soldiers' swords caused the death
of some brave trooper of the enemy.

Satisfied with driving the English Army into Portugal, Marshal
Marmont and General Dorsenne did not offer to pursue it beyond
Sabugal. This province was filled with English goods. It was the in-

stinct of the British to be closely attended by merchandise from their own country. At the same time, under one pretence or other, they contrived to destroy all competing local factories.

The army of Portugal fixed its quarters in the province of Leon, the general staff at Valladolid, and General Dorsenne returned with the troops of the Northern army toward Burgos. During our stay at Valladolid, Major de Vérigny received his well-deserved appointment as an officer of the Legion of Honour. When I congratulated him, he said:

"I am all the more pleased, my dear Parquin, at such complements coming from you, since you should feel rather annoyed that the marshal's request on your own behalf has failed to bring you the cross."

As he fixed the golden cross upon his breast, he added: "I would be delighted to place over your heart my own silver decoration. But do not despair: I shall renew my application for you at the first chance; and it shall not be very long unsuccessful, for I know that the marshal is extremely fond of you."

A few days later, on the 21st of February. 1812, I met with a great

sorrow. My leader, I might say my friend, Major de Vérigny, was mur-
dered by a soldier of the Valladolid garrison. On that day he had invited
me, with several officers of the escort and his nephew, M. Soufflot, a
young officer of our regiment, to a dinner which he gave in honour of
Major Thurot of the 1st Hussars, then passing through Valladolid on his
way to France and to the army of Russia. The repast had been a very
merry one, and at its close the guests returned to their rooms. Major

de Vérigny and his nephew were walking toward the latter's quarters, when as they were crossing the Arcade of the square, in the darkness of the night—it was about half past ten—they were rudely hustled by two *gendarmes* of the garrison, who had been keeping rather late hours in a wine-shop. The men answered impudently the first remonstrance of M. Soufflot, who had called to them to look out how they walked.

One of them, who was rather drunk, retraced his steps, and pulled out his sabre. The major who was in undress uniform and had no side arms, put his hand upon the hilt of his nephew's sabre, exclaiming:

"Let me deal with that man, Jules."

But M. Soufflot had quickly drawn his sabre from the scabbard, and was crying indignantly:

"What, scoundrel; you dare to attack a colonel!"

Just at that moment the *gendarme* swung his weapon, grazed young Soufflot's shoulder, and directing a vicious lunge toward the unfortunate major, who was advancing unarmed, thrust the sword into that gallant officer's body. The major fell at once, crying out: "Hold me, Jules; I am dying." And terrible to relate, in spite of the prompt attentions of the surgeon-major, his life could not be saved.

The murderer was at once traced, in obedience to Marshal Marmont's orders, and was arrested next morning. His trial was an affair of but a few hours and he was shot before we left Valladolid. We rendered military honours to Major de Vérigny, who was buried in the cathedral itself, his

brother, M. de la Chasse de Vérigny, captain in the Engineer corps, who afterward became a general and the commander of the Royal Military Staff School, being in charge of the funeral. Strange to say he also was doomed to die at the hand of an assassin—the criminally famous Fieschi.

During the month of April, 1812, Marshal Marmont started to the rescue of Ciudad-Rodrigo, which the English were again besieging. We hoped to reach the city in time, but its fortifications were so rickety and General Wellington so dexterously managed to gain inside assistance, that his troops had but to scale the walls and take possession of the place. Marshal Marmont arrived next morning and came up so close to the city that his escort suffered much damage by a cannonade from the batteries on the ramparts. A few men and horses were killed and Captain Laroche of the Élite company of the 11th Dragoons was wounded in the thigh by a bursting shell.

The Marshal Duke of Ragusa was compelled to leave in his rear the city of Ciudad-Rodrigo, while we undertook the task of pursuing' the English army, whose rearguard was formed by a Portuguese division under command of General Beresford. We came up with these troops in the Mondego valley. Major Denys, who later assumed the name of Damrémont, and who had been appointed to succeed M. de Vérigny in command of the escort, surprised this division at the head of his two hundred Élite horse. The weather was favourable for a cavalry attack, while a heavy rain interfered with the fire of the infantry. The English general had massed his troops in squares but they could not resist our charge. The first square being crushed in carried disorder to the others, when the men broke ranks and fled toward the woods—these being so near at hand that they served as a complete shelter against the pursuit of our cavalry.

During this charge I got a sabre-cut at an officer who stood in the midst of a square and who carried the flag of the Eurillas Regiment, the streamers of which bore the numerals "1808," which was doubtless the date of the formation of this corps. The officer hurriedly surrendered his ensign, imploring as he did so for mercy in these terms:

"*Nos la mata,*" words which mean: "Don't kill me."

The square we had just demolished was formed by a regiment reputed among the best. The four other flags of the division were also taken by the marshal's escort. Lieutenant Dubar of the 11th Dragoons, Second-Lieutenant Soufflot of the 20th Chasseurs and two privates rode forward, each with the flag he had captured in his hands. General Beresford caused to be inserted in the order of next day—as may be read in the French *Official Gazette*, which copied it from the English papers of the period—that the only flag the division still possessed would be stored at Oporto, and that the Portuguese must march without standards until they captured from the French an equal number!

Five flags, five hundred prisoners, and a number of dead—such was the result of this day's fighting, the victors only comprising two hundred of our Élite cavalry.

About four o'clock in the afternoon, while crossing a deserted village at the head of the escort, I noticed, not without surprise, in the

middle of the roadway, and in imminent danger of being trampled under our horses' feet, a male child almost completely nude. I had the column "oblique" to the right and ordered the trumpeter who rode near me to dismount and lift this innocent creature from its dangerous position. We wrapped the baby in our handkerchiefs, and I had it laid down again under a large porch. I was pleased to notice when I returned about six o'clock to the village, after the splendid charge I have just narrated, that the baby was no longer there. I hope that some charitable person took it in hand.

The army of Portugal re-entered Spain and we took our position behind the Douro River. We crossed that stream in the middle of July when the English again invaded Spain.

On the 11th of July, a few leagues beyond Salamanca., the Marshal Duke of Ragusa and some officers of his staff were reconnoitring near the enemy's line, when an English officer, riding beyond the scouts of his army, caracoled his horse almost in front of our outposts.

"What does that officer want?" inquired the Duke of Ragusa.

Being adjutant-major of the escort, I answered:

"My lord, that officer is evidently desirous of exchanging a few sabre-cuts with one of us, and if I were not on duty near the person of Your Excellency—"

"Is that all?" replied the marshal: "then you have my full permission, sir."

The words had hardly been uttered when I spurred my horse to a gallop and was soon quite close to the English officer. I parried the sabre-cut he aimed at me and returned it by a vigorous point-thrust which felled him to the earth. Passing the blade of my sabre quickly through his horse's bridle I led back the animal into our ranks, being welcomed by the hearty plaudits of the marshal and his *aides-de-camp*. A few minutes later I sent back the Englishman his saddle-bags, with an inquiry as to his condition. I was pleased to learn that his wound, although severe, was not likely to prove mortal.

His friends returned thanks for my restoration of the saddle-bags untouched, and further begged that I would sell them the horse, for which they offered forty guineas, at the same time informing me that it was not a thoroughbred. That may be." I answered, "but I feel like riding an English horse, and with your kind permission I will keep this one."

Between the 16th and 23rd of July the marshal concentrated his army in the plain that divides Salamanca from Alba de Tormès, whither he also summoned the Bonnet division, which occupied the Asturian provinces. General Dorsenne had lately succumbed to an attack of lock-jaw. The Imperial Guard, which he commanded in Spain, had set out by forced marches to take part in the Russia campaign. General Carrié was wounded and a prisoner. The intrepid General Montbrun had left Spain to meet a glorious death upon the battlefield of the Moskowa. The only commander that remained to lead our cavalry was General Curto, a good enough officer on the parade-ground but without that prestige which wins the unhesitating confidence of soldiers. Besides, our mounted troops at the time did not exceed two thousand strong, while the English cavalry was almost twice as numerous. Otherwise the forces of the two armies were about equal—that is, in infantry and artillery, except that the English had in their train a few thousand Spanish volunteers.

The Duke of Ragusa, our commander, was really a talented general. He was very brave and was greatly beloved for the good care he took of his soldiers. His division generals were all officers of high merit, as their names will suffice to prove, they being no other than Generals Foy, Clausel, Ferrey, Maucune and Bonnet. The brigadier-generals almost equalled them in reputation and in bravery, and for that matter the whole army was but too anxious to meet the Britons in the open field. Therefore the order of the day which was issued by Marshal Marmont on the 22nd of July, and which I read myself to the two hundred riders of the escort, produced on everybody an excellent impression.

In it the Marshal reminded his troops that the English Army, which for the last two years never faced us except when backed by armed breastworks, had suddenly changed its tactics; that it had at last decided to come up to the scratch and fight us at close quarters and that the emperor, although now five hundred leagues away from the army of Portugal, was intently observing the brave men that composed it. the marshal added that he had united his army to march against the English and do them battle to the cry of "Long live the Emperor."

The British have named this contest the Battle of Salamanca; the French call it the Battle of the Arapilés, the name of two conspicuous mountains distant from each other about a cannon's range. These eminences are situated in the middle of the plain where we fought the whole day long. One was at the extreme edge of the English formation and was occupied by General Wellington and his staff. The other was right in the middle of our lines. Marshal Marmont and his staff, leaving their horses below, had climbed to the top of the latter. Toward eleven o'clock of this beautiful summer day, the Duke of Ragusa, with field-glass in his hand, was intently surveying the English position. His butler had just spread upon the grass the silver tableware containing the marshal's cold breakfast, and His Excellency, with his *aides-de-camp* and chief of staff, were about sitting down to a comfortable meal, when some shells discharged from hand-mortars on the opposite mountain terminated very abruptly the luncheon not quite begun. The English commander had masked the battery of these pieces by interposing an infantry battalion, which he at once removed out of the way when the firing began. Falling into our mountain position entirely unexpected the projectiles forced us to hurry down to the plain to recover our horses. I had already mounted when I heard the Duke of Ragusa's voice loudly calling out: "Nicolas, Nicolas, my horse!" Nicolas was His Excellency's chief groom, but he did not happen to be at hand when the marshal reached the plain. I at once dismounted and offered my horse to the duke, who accepted it on account of the critical circumstances. He had already put a foot in the stirrup when the groom rushed forward, leading by the bridle his master's charger. The commander returned me my horse and started on a gallop to reach the line of battle, having first, however, given me the order to ride over to General Foy and direct him to bring his division forward. I at once fulfilled the mission confided to me.

As I was returning to the escort I noticed a number of men and horses of my own regiment, from which I had been absent for so long a time. Yielding to the natural desire to obtain some news of my former friends I rode over to a group of *chasseurs* who were holding the bridles of relief horses.

"What are you doing here?" I inquired of Narbonne, an officer of the 13th Chasseurs whom I found comfortably seated near the sutler's wagon, holding a sausage in one hand and a bottle of brandy in the other.

"Can't you see, dear comrade?" he coolly answered, "I am having my breakfast. Don't you wish to join me?"

"Sorry I must refuse," I said, "but I am in a great hurry. Just pass over the bottle that I may wet my whistle, for it is terribly hot today."

After gulping down a draught of brandy I thanked him, adding as I returned the flask:

"You are mighty well off in here; the cannonballs won't reach you. Do you belong to the army transport?"

"My dear Parquin, do you want me to fight against those English who were so kind to my family and self when we took refuge in England in '93? I could not even think of being so ungrateful. If people want me to fight," he added, trying to appear as ferocious as he could, "let them put me in front of some other nation—the Austrians for example!"

"Oh, that's it!" I said, bursting into a laugh and spurring my horse to the gallop, "I suppose you would like to pick what we call a German quarrel with those other fellows?"

This Narbonne was a young man from the noble St. Germain suburb, and when one day galloping rather close to the emperor, who was driving to Malmaison, managed to fling dust into His Majesty's carriage. Next morning he received his brevet as second-lieutenant and was sent to the army, where he never raised the slightest dust of any kind, for no useful service could be got out of him. Finally he was sent back home and I believe that since then he became insane.

Marshal Marmont, in imitation of the English general, had some

light artillery carried by hand to the top of his own mountain, and there finally established his headquarters for the day. Not having need of any escort on this vantage-ground he ordered our major, M. Denys, to lead his two hundred troopers wherever they might be found useful. The major placed us at once in array, at the right of the 3rd Hussars, where we stood for a whole hour under the fire of the enemy's artillery, which did us some damage. Finally we were relieved from this uncomfortable position and were delighted to receive the order to charge a regiment of heavy cavalry wearing the historic scarlet coats. I was just returning from this charge when I observed, not over a hundred paces from me, a *chasseur* of the 20th Regiment, also a member of the escort, who was closely pursued by two English soldiers.

"Face the enemy, *chasseur*," I cried out, as I rushed to his assistance.

But the *chasseur* didn't stop, and one of the English cavalrymen, who had evidently lost control of his steed, tilted violently against the right flank of mine, so that both horses fell together. Then the second English rider quickly approached calling to me:

"Prisoner! You are my prisoner," and directing me with his sabre to march in front of him.

The memory of the time when I was a prisoner in Russia suddenly came back to me, and noticing that my antagonist failed to make use of his pistols, I myself strained every nerve to ward off his sabre-cuts, having first managed to crawl from under my horse, which at once darted wildly away toward the escort. I was fencing vigorously to get

a cut at the legs of my adversary's horse, when the return of my own steed to the escort without me caused two of our men to ride out to my assistance. Seeing me engaged on foot with an enemy who was mounted they rushed toward us at full gallop. As soon as he saw them coming the Englishman gave up the fight, but not before aiming at my wrist a vicious sabre-cut. Happily my leather gauntlet was so thick as to weaken the blow, otherwise I should certainly have had my hand cleft off. In the ardour of conflict—I was hardly twenty-five years old at the time—I thought little of the blow, but as I lifted my hand on the

saddle-peak to again mount horse I became conscious that my right wrist was utterly powerless. Accordingly I had to mount on the wrong side, and galloped off at once—not even taking time to pick up my colback—only too well pleased to escape with so slight a wound.

When we reached the spot whence the two *chasseurs* had started to my rescue, we found only a single horseman, who was instructed to tell us that the escort had hastened along to the foot of the mountain, where the general-in-chief was said to be lying severely wounded. From there we had to proceed to the ambulance, which was established in the city of Alba de Tormès. The journey was over a league long, of which the greater part was through thick woods. We put our horses to a gallop and yet had barely the time to reach our friends, for the swarming cavalry of the enemy managed to outride our left wing and were pushing in the direction of the La Tormès bridge. Lieutenant-General Maucune fortunately noticed this movement and by throwing some troops into the woods cut off the advance of the English in that direction.

I had lost so much blood while galloping, having the sabre hanging

from my wrist by its sword-knot, that I should certainly have fainted right out of the saddle if my *chasseurs* had not noticed the danger and lifted me to the ground. The enemy was coming closer and closer and everything seemed to indicate that we were losing the battle. The *chasseurs* had nothing with which to revive my strength and could only splash on my face, while I still remained prostrate and insensible, some water from a neighbouring brook. Suddenly these words: "What a pity it is to abandon our brave officer to the enemy!" pierced my drowsy

brain and caused me to open my eyes. On noticing this the *chasseurs* exclaimed: "Cheer up, adjutant-major," and then almost carrying me, placed me again on horseback. It was past six o'clock when we crossed the bridge and at last entered the city of Alba de Tormès.

The marshal had arrived there at four o'clock. Although very serious his wound was not mortal. A shell had crushed his right arm and broken two of his ribs. The surgeons concluded not to risk the amputation of the arm, while knowing it must remain forever useless. General Clausel took command of the army and by his able manoeuvring saved it from further disaster. Toward midnight the Foy division, which had been kept in reserve, was massed into a square and proved a rampart against the enemy, who must also have been very thankful that the Duke of Ragusa, who had postponed attacking them for seven days, did not delay doing so just one day more—King Joseph and Marshal Soult having in fact now arrived to help him, with an army of forty thousand of whom ten thousand were cavalry.

All things considered the English had to pay dear for their small victory. On our side there was mourning for the deaths of Generals Ferey and Thomières, and of Colonel Jardet, one of the marshal's *aides-de camp*. We retreated in good order toward Valladolid and Burgos, an English division following us closely without attempt-

ing to interfere, with the movement. The wound of our general-in-chief gave him extreme pain, so that he could not endure either horseback or carriage. His surgeon arranged to have him transported on a litter, carried by mules, one harnessed in front and one behind; but the uneven gait of the animals gave him so many shocks that the duke got out of temper from the suffering they caused him. When this became known among the escort our *chasseurs* at once volunteered to carry the litter upon their shoulders. For that purpose twenty-four men dismounted, out of nearly two hundred who composed the escort. Twelve of these became bearers of the two forward shafts and the same number took hold of the two rear ones. These twenty-four men were relieved by as many of their comrades whenever they showed signs of fatigue. Thus was the long march rendered less painful for the duke, and after taking brief rests at Valladolid, Burgos, and Vittoria, in the month of September he finally reached Bayonne, where he found *Madame la Maréchale*, this devoted lady having hastened from the baths of Aix, in Savoy, on hearing the first news of the Battle of Arapilés and of her husband's serious disablement.

The marshal thanked the escort for the attentions it had shown him and sent the troops back to their respective regiments.

I had been enabled myself to ride the whole distance to Bayonne with my right arm in a sling, though indeed my wound was far from being healed. Accordingly I was sent to the depot of the regiment, located then at Niort. The squadrons of the 20th Chasseurs, to which I belonged, had just been incorporated in the 13th Chasseurs. It was not without emotions of regret that I left the regiment I had first joined as a volunteer, and which I cherished dearly: but the 20th Chasseurs was now to take part in the Russian expedition, and thus it was found necessary to detach from it the squadrons which had been designated to serve with the army of Portugal.

CHAPTER 4

Germany & France
1813-1814

Arriving at Niort in the month of October, 1812, it was not very long ere I became a sufferer from rheumatism—brought about by the several wounds I had received in the Polish campaign of 1807, the Wagram campaign of 1809, and finally in the unfortunate Spanish war.

During this latest campaign the bivouacs I shared in had never any warmer bedding than chopped straw, and that doubtless contributed not a little to my painful affection. I petitioned the War Minister for a furlough as a means to recover my health. As soon as it was granted I went on to Paris, where I spent the winter with my own family. There I found my married sisters and my brother, the barrister, who was already beginning to gain a standing in his profession. Later he became very eminent as a lawyer.

The emperor arrived suddenly in Paris on the 19th of December, 1812. He had caused himself to be preceded by his twenty-ninth bulletin, which was fully as sensational as those of the Battles of Eylau and Essling.

It was the custom of the emperor frequently to review the troops

254

that were garrisoned in Paris. On the 6th of March, 1813, I went out of sheer curiosity to witness such a review, and observing on the Place Carrousel General Lefèbvre-Desnouettes, the colonel of the horse *chasseurs* of the Guard, I approached him with the request to be permitted to serve in his regiment.

"Well, my dear comrade," the general said to me, after asking several questions which I readily answered, "do you know anyone who feels an interest in you and who can recommend you to me?"

Just at that moment I noticed the Marshal Duke of Ragusa, with his arm in a,sling. He had stepped out of his carriage and was about to enter the Tuileries courtyard.

"There, general," I exclaimed, "there is my Lord Duke of Ragusa, under whose orders I served in Spain; will you be kind enough to ask him what he thinks of me?"

General Lefèbvre-Desnouettes graciously consented to walk toward the marshal and to refer my name to him. The duke, as soon as he saw me and heard my name, beckoned me toward him, and right in my presence he thus addressed the general:

"Take this officer into your regiment, general: take him by all means; you will secure a most valuable acquisition in him."

A few days later I was in receipt of my brevet as lieutenant in the horse *chasseurs* of the Old Guard.

On the 6th of April, 1813, I was present in full uniform at the head of my squad, which paraded as a part of two squadrons of the regiment. It was the occasion of one of those reviews which were so often held by the emperor in the Tuileries courtyard, after his return from the Russian campaign. I was yearning to have a brief conversation with His Majesty, but was afraid lest I should miss the chance, because he usually hurried by when in front of his Guides without stopping to address them. Therefore I dismounted when the squadrons were ordered to "parade rest," and went over to take position at the left of the Young Guard Infantry corps, which His Majesty was just then inspecting.

"Who are you?" demanded the emperor, when he reached the spot where I had planted myself.

"I am an officer of your Old Guard, Sire; I have stepped down one rank to serve near to the person of Your Majesty."

"What do you want of me?"

"I want the cross."

"What have you done to earn it?"

"I am a native of Paris; I left it as a volunteer when barely sixteen. I have passed through eight campaigns; I won my epaulets on the battlefield and I have received ten wounds, which I certainly would not exchange for those I gave the enemy. I also captured a battle-flag in Portugal; the general-in-chief at that time proposed me for the cross; but it is so far from Moscow to Portugal that the answer has not yet arrived."

"Never mind; I am here to give it to you myself! Berthier, enter down the name of this officer for the cross, and let his brevet be delivered to him tomorrow. I don't wish to be any longer in such a brave fellow's debt."

And that was how I received the cross of the Legion of Honour.

I was so exultant that when I went over to my squad I mentioned the glad news to several officers of the regiment, who had also but lately joined the Guard, having left the army of Spain without receiv-

ing the cross. Lieutenant Goudemetz immediately followed my example, and approaching the emperor begged him to grant him the cross.

"What have you done to deserve it?"

"Sire, my two brothers and myself enlisted as volunteers, ten years ago, in the 3rd Hussars. I believe that the services which they and I have rendered to Your Majesty merit the decoration."

"Ah, you really think so?" queried the emperor.

"Yes, Sire, I do, and the more so that both my brothers have been killed and I remain alone, youngest of three, in the service of our country."

"Note this officer for the cross," said the emperor, visibly affected, turning round to the Prince of Neufchâtel.

A third officer introduced himself, and was asked the same question. His name was Legontz-Duplessis, and he replied to the emperor:

"Sire, at the Battle of Talavera, in Spain, being then a sergeant in the 5th Dragoons, I captured the standard of the Walloon Guards, killed the officer who bore it, and routed the escort that surrounded him. For this feat of arms I was placed upon the order of the day."

"It was splendid, indeed," said the emperor, smiling, "but who is to assure me that all this is true?"

"Your *aide-de-camp* here present, Sire, General Corbineau, who was colonel of the regiment and also led the identical charge."

General Corbineau nodded affirmatively, and Legontz-Duplessis received the cross. After the review, the emperor provided the troops out of his own purse with an extra meal and rations of wine, further inviting the officers to dine with him at six in the evening. Two hundred officers of all arms of the service, who had taken part in the review, met at this banquet, which was spread on the Feuillants' Terrace in the garden of the Tuileries. There were four tables

of fifty covers each, presided over respectively by Generals Lemarrois, Lauriston, Lobau, and Rapp, all *aides-de camp* of the emperor and for that occasion his representatives to do the honours in his name. It may well be imagined that the banquet was a merry one. Toasts were proposed successively to the emperor, the empress and the King of Rome. A number of officers present had lately been promoted, or had been

awarded the cross; others, younger in the service, had similar honours in prospect. The opportunity to win them was not very remote, for on the following day we got marching orders for the army of Germany.

And true there were many among us who ate on that day, the 6th of April, 1813, their last festive meal in the shadow of the Tuileries.

Next morning I received three thousand *francs* from the quartermaster of my regiment, as bounty money in the Guard. This allowance was made to officers to help purchase the regimental uniform and accoutrements, which were both very elaborate and costly.

On the 10th of April I left Paris with a detachment of my regiment for a march across France to join the army of Germany, commanded by the emperor himself. In passing through a certain city in Champagne I had an amusing experience which might be attributed somewhat to the virtues of the local wine.

It was a custom for many years with the officer of the Guard *chasseurs*, whenever they stopped at E———, to dine in a body at the hotel de l'Écu, and there drink the native brands to the health of the emperor.

At noon I entered my designated lodging, which was in a house on the main street pertaining to a rich widow. I had just gone to my room, being still covered with the dust of the road, when a tall and handsome girl stepped in with some refreshments on a tray and conveyed to me the apologies of the owner of the house of whom I had naturally sent in my card. This lady intimated that she was very sorry to have to miss my call by being obliged to visit her lawyer on pressing business. I returned my thanks for her courtesy but gave the matter no further thought, while I gallantly observed to the young woman that brought the refreshments:

"May I ask your name, *Mademoiselle?* for you are decidedly the handsomest person I have seen in this town."

Not answering the last remark, which impelled her to blush and laugh at the same time, she retorted quickly:

"My name is Adèle, Mr. Officer, and I am *Madame's* housemaid, quite at your service if you have need of anything."

"I shall test the offer, Miss Adèle, by trespassing on your kindness right away. Will you be so good as to sew a new ribbon to my cross of the Legion of Honour, as I find that the old one has become rather faded." The *demoiselle* took the ribbon in her hands and ran out of my room to accomplish the task. A few minutes later she returned with my cross. She was gracious enough to place it back upon my dolman; then, quick as a flash, she pressed her lips upon the portrait of the emperor, as one might do to the picture of a beloved friend.

"Ah, ha," I exclaimed, quite touched by her enthusiasm, "you appear to be very devoted to the emperor."

"Indeed I am, Mr. Officer," replied the warm-hearted girl, "and if I were a man the emperor would have no more loyal servant."

This truly French sentiment made me an admirer of Mademoi-

260

selle Adèle, and I watched every opportunity for further conversation with her.

At dinner time I went over to the hotel to meet my comrades. As usual, the meal was boisterously merry.

On returning to the lodgings I met Adèle in the act of leaving my room, where we at once began a cordial chat. Just as the talk became animated we were startled by an angry tapping at the entrance of the corridor.

"What is it, *Madame*," asked Adèle; "do you need me?"

"No. *Mademoiselle*, I do not need you; but I notice you have strange company while about your duties."

Adèle replied with perfect coolness: "It is true, *Madame*, I am not alone; but it is not Mr. G—— who is here."

She had no sooner uttered these words than we heard the lady of the house walk testily away.

"Please tell me," I said to Adèle, "what is the meaning of this little bit of comedy?"

"Certainly I will, Mr. Officer, for you don't belong to our city, and therefore will not make scandal. The gentleman whose name I mentioned is *Madame's* favourite admirer, and I often have occasion to receive him privately into the house. He is in the country today, and that is why she is alone and displays so much peevishness at the enjoyment of others."

I then inquired of Adèle if she would have any need to excuse herself on my account and for the sharp retort to her mistress. She answered:

"Oh, don't you worry, Mr. Officer: *Madame* is too kind to bear me a grudge very long, and besides, it is not to her interest to do so. She may be a little moody for a couple of days, but that's all."

I immediately left the sprightly girl, promising to remember her as a true and sturdy little Frenchwoman.

I was just mounting my horse next morning when I noticed, with surprise, for it was still very early, the mistress of the house gathering roses in a little garden off the courtyard. Not having actually met her on the previous day, it would now have been poor etiquette to omit paying her my compliments. I therefore congratulated her upon her early rising, observing that it was a sign of excellent health. The widow, who was really quite handsome and had a brilliant complexion, politely asked me how I had enjoyed my night's repose.

"Very much, indeed, *Madame*," I replied; "only the champagne I had quaffed with my comrades rather disturbed the beginning of my sleep. An enchanting dream, however, aided me to round out an invigorating night's rest."

With these ceremonious words I made a low bow and withdrew, inwardly congratulating M. G————.upon his good taste, for the lady was indeed an attractive person.

We continued our march to the east and passed the frontier at Strasburg on the 1st of May. On the 10th of the same month we reached Dresden. The regiment of mounted *chasseurs* of the Guard

were quartered in the villages adjoining the city. Among the officers of the corps was a major named Lion, an old acquaintance of mine, for he had served as captain in the 10th Chasseurs. He welcomed me very kindly and to him I owed the favour of being placed in charge of a squad of the 10th company, commanded by his brother-in-law, Captain Klein de Kleinenberg, one of the best cavalry officers I ever met in my military career. Later on he became a general. On the 12th of May we witnessed the entrance of the King of Saxony into his own capital, which he had left on the approach of the allied troops.

The emperor, at the head of the division of his grenadier and mounted Guard, rode out to meet the king about a quarter of a league

beyond the city. He had sent his *aide-de*-camp, General Count de Fla-
haut, as far as Pirna to compliment the monarch on his return to
Saxony. On the 20th of May took place the Battle of Bautzen and
the capture of the city so named. Next day the Battle of Wurschen
was won, which as well as the first had been against the armies of the
coalition. The lack of cavalry unfortunately deprived us of the fruit of
these two days' victories, which like the battles in Egypt were exclusively won by artillery and infantry.

From the 20th to the 30th of May my men and I belonged to the
squadron of horse *chasseurs* on duty—better known during service as
the Emperor's Guides. His Majesty always kept near to him, in actual

campaign, four squadrons from the different branches of the Old Guard cavalry. and these he would occasionally hurl upon the enemy in critical moments. It was on one of these occasions, at the village of Gilly, being the eve of the Battle of Quatre-Bras in 1815, that the brave General Letort charged furiously with the two squadrons on duty and routed and captured two Prussian battalions, which had

formed the square, with an added trophy of five cannon. Unfortunately General Letort was killed in this charge, the army losing in him one of its most brilliant officers.

The squadron of horse *chasseurs* had likewise to perform a service personal to the emperor. A lieutenant, one sergeant, two corporals, twenty-two *chasseurs* and a trumpeter constantly rode at the front be-

hind His Majesty. A corporal and four *chasseurs*, one of whom carried
the notebook and another the field-telescope of His Majesty galloped
before the emperor and cleared the way for him. Should he stop or
dismount the *chasseurs* would at once do likewise, fixing the bayonets
to their carbines and forming a square with the emperor in the middle. The officer in command of this escort-squad always rode close to

the emperor's person; only King Murat and the Prince of Neufchâtel were allowed nearer to his Imperial Majesty.

Should the emperor occupy quarters the officer on duty would keep watch in the room adjoining. In this case the *chasseurs* dismounted and ranged in front of the house, holding their horses' bridles. Besides there was always at hand one of the emperor's own steeds, saddled and bridled, with two attendant grooms. The escort-squad was relieved every two hours, so that at each minute of the day or night the same

number of men were always ready for instant action. The first person the emperor's eye fell upon, as he left his room, was the officer of the escort. The post was one of great honour and absolute confidence. This troop showed the greatest devotion to the emperor, and its officers and men were ever generously rewarded. Thus, there were always four *chasseurs* from each company of each regiment of the Old Guard, who besides the cross of the Legion of Honour, and sometimes the badge of the Iron Crown, which brought with it a pension of two

hundred and fifty *francs* a year, were given pensions upon the canals or upon the Mt. Napoleon of Milan, and were thus in receipt of as much as eight hundred *francs* a year. It is needless to say that among these brave soldiers His Majesty never found an ungrateful heart. Of the numerous deeds of loyalty for which the Guard *chasseurs* were so famed I wish to mention one that I thought specially admirable.

On the 18th of October, 1813, at Leipzig, a *chasseur* of my squad of the class mentioned above—that is, fully pensioned and decorated—was missing from the ranks, having had his horse killed during the day. I thought that he had been sent back to the regimental depot to get a new mount; his absence in that case would have lasted about ten days. What was my surprise next morning—everybody knows that the Battle of Leipzig lasted three days—to see him in the ranks again mounted on a superb horse with a closely trimmed tail. When I questioned him, he said gravely:

"Lieutenant, when a man has been endowed by His Majesty, the Emperor and King, he has always in his belt a year's salary to purchase a horse with, and thus not miss the glory of being killed in His Majesty's service. If I be unlucky enough during this campaign to have a second horse killed, then I shall have to go to my regiment to procure another. The horse I mount now I bought yesterday out of my own money, from an officer in the Dragoon Guards who won't need it any longer, for he has just had a leg cut off."

"And what did you pay for it?"

"Twenty-five *louis*."

The emperor, who was perfectly well aware of the devotion of his Guides, often allowed them to make remarks that would have been severely punished coming from any other source. One day an escort *chasseur* fell while he was galloping in front of His Majesty, and the man was picking himself up as best he could when the emperor, passing him at full speed, called him a blundering fellow. The words were scarcely spoken when His Majesty's own horse, which had not been properly curbed by its rider, rolled in the dust with the great man. Whilst the emperor, assisted by his equerry, was mounting another horse, the *chasseur*, who had resumed his saddle, galloped past to reach the vanguard and shouted loud enough for His Majesty to hear:

"It seems I am not the only blunderer today!"

On the 2nd of May, at four o'clock in the morning, the Guard cavalry—the Red Lancers—with General Colbert at their head, and a division of Saxon *cuirassiers* commanded by General Latour-Mau-

bourg, pursued the Prussians and Russians along the road to Silesia and captured a number of stragglers, wagons, and ammunition carts. The Russian artillery, however, inflicted much damage on the Saxons. One officer of the Guide regiment was wounded in the hand by a fragment of shell: his name was Lantivy. A great loss to the army was that of General Bruyères, killed by a cannonball which shattered both his legs. He was an excellent cavalry officer and had served through the Egyptian campaign. During this same battle the emperor, noticing a *chasseur* of his escort struck dead by a cannonball, quite near to him, observed to the Grand Marshal, who was approaching:

"Duroc, fortune is unkind to us today."

Only two hours later fortune aimed a more cruel blow right at the emperor's heart.

When His Majesty left the village of Reichenbach he continued his way towards Goerlitz, where he expected to spend the night. Just as he was rapidly descending the hollow road that crossed the village, a spent cannonball ricocheted from a tree and slew on the spot General Kirgener of the engineers, besides tearing into the abdomen of General Duroc. Both these officers had turned away almost fifty paces from the road, on the right side, to water their chargers at a small pond they had observed there. An officer of the Élite *gendarmes* saw General Kirgener struck down from his horse, and hastened with the painful news to the emperor. A minute later another *aide-de-camp* informed His Majesty that the Grand Marshal had been dangerously wounded. At the first word of this officer the emperor retorted sharply:

"You are mistaken, sir; you are speaking of General Kirgener. I was told of his death a moment ago."

"Sire," persisted the officer, "it is only too true that the same cannonball has struck both these generals. The death of General Kirgener was instantaneous, and the Grand Marshal has just been carried in a hopeless condition into the house of the village rector."

Just then Colonel Gourgand's chief *aide de-camp* galloped up to the emperor, to advise him that the Prince of Moskowa's movement on Goerlitz had proved a success. Without answering a single word the emperor retraced his steps, entered the pastor's house and walked straight to the bed on which Grand Marshal Duroc was laid. A battalion of the Old Guard at once bivouacked as an escort around the manse, while the four squadrons on duty were quartered in the neighbouring village of Markersdorff.

We left this fatal spot next day, the 23rd of May. The emperor granted a yearly income of twelve hundred *francs* to the Protestant rector, and also gave him a sum of money equal to the value of his house, under condition that he erect and preserve on the location of the Grand Marshal's bed, a tablet on which should appear the following inscription, dictated by His Majesty in person:

The General Duroc, Duc de Frioul.

Grand Marshal of the palace to Emperor Napoleon,
Having been struck by a cannonball
Expired here in the arms of his sovereign and friend.

The Pleiswitz armistice being signed we were quartered on the 4th of June in the neighbourhood of Dresden. Lodgings for the emperor were chosen inside the city and his headquarters were established in the Marcolini Palace. On the 10th of August the whole Guard was reviewed by him and on the same day was held the Fête-Napoleon. Over fifty thousand soldiers were present in that review—artillery, infantry and cavalry.

As the emperor rode down along the ten lines formed by the troops, he failed not to lift his hat whenever he heard the shouts of "Long live the Emperor!" He furthermore answered them by the cry of "*Vive la France!*" Nor need I omit to mention that pay for the month of August was duplicated to all the officers of the Old Guard. The Fête-Napoleon was celebrated five days in advance because hostilities had been re-

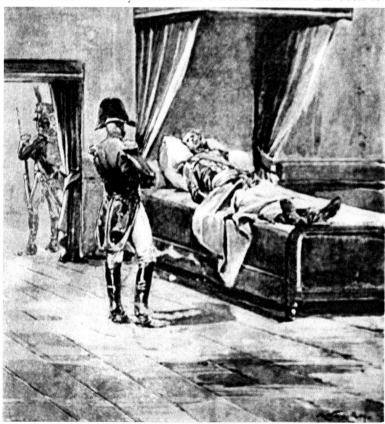

sumed by General Blucher, in criminal violation of the laws of war—
the 17th having been the day agreed on by both contestants.

On the 14th of August we struck tents to enter Dresden and next
day left that city with the emperor at our head to open another campaign in the direction of Bautzen. On the same day M. de Narbonne,
one of the emperor's *aides-de-camp*, returned from Vienna bringing with him the declaration of war by Austria against France. Thus
another of the great powers was pitted against us. The allied troops
amounted to five hundred thousand men, while we had no more
than three hundred thousand soldiers besides the Imperial Guard. But
wasn't our emperor there?

On the 21st, at Löwenberg, General Maison's corps drove before
it the Prussians under General York, who had taken possession of the
town. On his side Marshal Marmont defeated General Sacken's division and forced it out of Bautzen, while Marshal Macdonald threatened the centre of Blucher's army and forced that commander to
begin a retreat. Thus did the French Army vigorously follow up its
successes and compel the Prussians to take refuge behind the Katzbach. Finally, on the 23rd, the emperor routed Blucher so completely
at Goldberg as absolutely to drive him back into Silesia. Blucher's son,
who served as one of his father's *aides*, was captured and brought to
the emperor by one of the Mameluke guards. His Majesty at once sent
him home to Berlin on parole.

Satisfied with this repulse of the Prussian Army, the emperor ordered his Guard to counter-march and return to the vicinity of Dres-

den, which was reached on the 26th of August at ten in the morning. It was not an hour too soon, for the Austrian Army had already crossed the Erzgebirge Mountains and was encamped before Dresden, two hundred thousand strong, with Prince Von Schwartzenberg in the chief command. On the same day, at four o'clock in the afternoon, the prince assailed at all points the Dresden suburbs. These were gallantly defended; several officers of the Guard were wounded, among them being General Gros, so noted for his bravery and for his pungent repartee whenever addressed by the emperor.

One day in a teasing mood His Majesty told him, as he was inspecting the drill of some troops on the Champ de Mars:

"Gros, the grenadiers handle their guns better than the *chasseurs*."

The general replied: "I will wager you six *francs*, Sire, that my *chasseurs* drill better than your grenadiers."

They tell of a courtier at the Tuileries, who once informed the emperor that General Gros of his Guard could not write decent French, nor even speak his mother tongue without blundering. The emperor answered: "I never noticed that Gros was such a bad French scholar on the battlefield."

Young Berenger, one of the emperor's *aides*, had his leg torn off by a cannonball as he came back from delivering an order in the suburbs. The enemy was nevertheless repulsed at all points and lost six thousand men, of whom four thousand were killed; but the day cost us three thousand men.

The same day, as I was crossing the main street of the Berg suburb, where my regiment had taken position, I was saluted by a corporal wearing the cross, a, member of the third company.

I returned his salute and was riding on without stopping, when he came over to me and said:

"Lieutenant, allow me to wish you good-day and to ask you how you are, for I happen to be an old acquaintance of yours. You probably don't recognize me?"

"I must admit that I do not recall your features," I answered him. "I have been only five months with the Guard *chasseurs*, and I know but a few of the men. What is your name, please?"

"I was the chief trumpeter of the 8th hussars," he answered, "whom you wounded by a sword-thrust in 1806, some ten leagues from Warsaw, in a duel we had there together."

"Oh," I exclaimed, "I remember you now very well. So you have given up your bugle and your regiment to serve in the Imperial Guard."

"I have lieutenant."

"I am greatly pleased to see you again; how long have you been in this corps?"

"Ever since the Russian campaign. I was promoted corporal a year ago."

"And what is the name of your captain?"

"M. Achintre."

"Oh, yes, I know him, and I shall be delighted to commend you to him. Meanwhile whenever you meet me, corporal, whether on the march or in bivouac, just come right over to me. I shall always have a drop of something good to share with you."

Alas, this poor fellow only once made use of the invitation thus tendered to him with such sincere goodwill. The next day was that of the Battle of Dresden and when I went over in the evening to Captain Achintre, to recommend the young man to him, I was distressed to hear that he had been killed by a cannonball.

"I deeply regret poor Auguste," said the captain to me, "for he was a most excellent soldier and I should certainly have promoted him to a sergeantcy in the company." He added: "the poor corporal returned last evening after his chat with you, Parquin, and was telling his comrades what a clever sword-thrust you administered him when you served as non-commissioned quartermaster in the same regiment. 'He was not like many other quartermasters,' he exclaimed, 'who only know how to write and keep accounts; he knew in addition how to use his sword properly!'"

"Poor Auguste!" I returned, "he will fight no more duels. He is now where we all are sure to follow him someday."

I took leave of Captain Achintre and returned to my squad.

The Battle of Dresden, which was so glorious an event for the French Army, yielded my regiment only a heavy rainstorm and a thick hail of cannonballs. Lieutenant Brice, paymaster of the regiment, had a magnificent horse killed under him. He would not have taken three thousand *francs* for it, and yet he parted with it for nothing, or rather he only received a first-class scolding from General Lefébvre-Desnouettes, who was not at all pleased to have his paymaster risk a battlefield when his duty was to be in Dresden with his books and cashbox.

Prince Murat's cavalry made a grand display of intrepidity: they charged in one mass and drove right through the centre of the enemy, already much shaken up by the fire of the Guard artillery. It was on that day that General Moreau, who rode among a group of the general officers of the allies, was struck dead a few feet from Czar Alexander. A Saxon peasant, to whose cottage the general was carried with both legs shattered by a cannonball, brought to the emperor about five o'clock a splendid Danish dog, bearing around its neck a wide copper band engraved with the words:

"I belong to General Moreau."

This peasant it was also who first gave news of Moreau's death, and offered to sell the dog for ten *napoleons*. The emperor had the amount paid him and ordered him to take away the dog.

Before General Moreau died he addressed to Czar Alexander these last and most significant words:

"Sire! Attack Emperor Napoleon wherever he is not!"

This advice was communicated to the allied generals and was but too exactly followed.

On the evening of the Battle of Dresden Major Desvas, a cousin of mine, who when captain in the Carbineers of the 25th Light Infantry had been wounded at the Battle of Arapilés, and whom I had the good fortune to bring back to France in one of the Duke of Ragusa's wagons, called to make me a visit on his way to the ambulance. He had received a bullet through the arm. I sent him to the lodgings I had occupied at Dresden in a clergyman's house. There he was welcomed and treated very decently. Unfortunately he belonged to the division that remained in Dresden, under Marshal Gouvion Saint-Cyr, and which was obliged to capitulate after the Leipzig campaign. This capitulation was not recognized by Prince Schwartzenberg and thirty thousand French soldiers were led prisoners into Austria contrary to all rules of honourable warfare.

This Battle of Dresden, which in the manoeuvring of the troops

the emperor used to compare with Jéna, also fought in Saxony seven years before, resulted in the complete rout of the Austrians, who lost thirty thousand men, of whom twelve thousand were prisoners, besides two hundred cannon, over one thousand military wagons, etc. The emperor slept on the battlefield and next morning entered Dresden at the head of his Guard. We continued our march toward Pirna without any stay. From Pirna we started back next day to Dresden, none of us knowing the cause for this retrograde movement. A rumour spread through the army that General Vandamme's corps had been fighting the whole Austrian force, which was then in full retreat toward Bohemia, and that the general had been made prisoner with seven thousand men after many feats of prodigious bravery.

The Guard then moved toward Berlin, beginning its march on the 7th of October. Two days later, however, we again returned to Dresden, from which we started on the 10th to rejoin the main body of the army at Leipzig. On the 13th the emperor bivouacked with his Guard about a quarter of a league from the last named city. I was in command of the squad of *chasseurs* on duty. About four o'clock I observed, trotting briskly toward us, a squadron of the Guard of Honour which was escorting the King of Saxony and his family from Dresden to Leipzig. As soon as the emperor noticed the signs of the approaching party, he walked about fifty paces along the road, and was going yet farther, to give welcome to the king, when the Saxon monarch came down from his carriage and advanced bare-headed to meet the emperor. I still seem to see the King of Saxony, a tall, handsome old man, with a shock of powdered hair and a queue. His dress was a white uniform and he carried two watches, the fobs of which hung down along his hips. He was taking off his gloves to offer his hand to the emperor when the latter embraced him and called him brother. The two sovereigns proceeded at once to the Queen of Saxony's carriage. The queen had on her left the Princess Augusta, her daughter, and I was so near the emperor, who spoke in a clear voice, that I could hear distinctly what he said to the two princesses.

"Sire," inquired the queen of him, "how are the empress and the King of Rome?"

"They are both well,'" answered the emperor, "I received a courier yesterday."

"You intend to give battle tomorrow, Sire?" asked the queen.

"I think so."

"And you shall win it!" exclaimed the Princess Augusta.

"That is spoken like a woman: women never doubt anything. However, we shall hope for the best."

The emperor saluted his august visitors, who then continued on their way to Leipzig, which city he himself was so soon to enter.

Prince Murat, with his dragoons of the army of Spain, had only just reached us across the French territory, and on that day, October

13th, they really performed wonders. The prince nearly lost his life, however, in one of those brilliant charges he was so fond of leading. In traversing a piece of swamp ground his horse's feet began to sink. He was on the point of being sabred down by a Russian officer, who certainly did not know with whom he had to deal, when the prince's groom observed his master's perilous position. This man, who had formerly been a dragoon, still carried his sabre, as he preferred it when campaigning to the hunting-knife which is usual with grooms. And he used that sabre so quickly that it was already plunged through the body of the Russian officer ere the latter found time to strike down our Ajax. The emperor conferred the cross on this devoted groom, who was also given a pension of six thousand *francs* by the City of Naples, as a recognition of his brilliant exploit on the battlefield of Leipzig.

On the 16th of October at nine in the morning began the action at Wachau, better known as the first day of the Battle of Leipzig. Three salvos were the signal given by the enemy, and immediately afterward they opened fire from two hundred cannon. The projectiles began to drop into our ranks like falling fruit. This explosion of artillery was intended to protect the three columns of Wittgenstein and Kleist on their advance to Wachau. The village was vigorously defended by the corps of General Lauriston. It was taken and retaken by the cavalry of General Latour-Maubourg, who, toward noon, had a leg carried off by a cannonball close to the same spot General Coehorn had both his legs shattered by a ball which passed beneath his horse. This day witnessed the deaths of General Vial and General Rochambeau, the latter an old comrade of La Fayette in the American war.

The Guard cavalry was formed in battle array about the centre of our army. I can still see General Drouot, on foot, directing with savage energy the fire from a battery of one hundred cannon of the Guard artillery. The emperor seeing there was danger to the extreme right wing, which had nineteen thousand men commanded by Marshal Oudinot, all from the infantry of the Young Guard, sent to its relief General Letort with eight hundred horse, composed of two hundred each of the *chasseurs*, lancers, dragoons and grenadiers of the Old Guard. The Duke of Reggio, as a precautionary measure, had formed his troops into hollow squares. It so happened that I was included in the cavalry column sent forward by the emperor. We trotted in squad formation toward the right wing. On reaching the ground we passed in between two infantry squares and at once formed up for action.

A charge of Austrian cavalry against us failed completely and even scored us a brilliant success. the position we had just assumed on the battlefield cut off the retreat of a regiment of horse, the Latour dragoons, who must needs pass our corps if they attempted to rejoin their lines. Marshal Oudinot, whose situation we had greatly improved, came out of one of the squares and suddenly appearing before our column, shouted:

"Cavalry, face about! here is a storm for you!"

And in fact at the very moment loomed up a cloud of dust, through which glittered sabres of the Latour dragoons, but we opposed such a wall of steel to them that one hundred and ninety out of their two hundred became our captives.

On this occasion I noticed Marshal Oudinot alone in the thick of the *mêlée* and in imminent danger, for in spite of every effort he could not succeed in pulling his sword out of the scabbard. I lost not a second in placing myself alongside the illustrious marshal and covering him with my body. His Excellency finally drew out the weapon and was soon safe again in the middle of one of his infantry squares. The same evening his son, who was a captain in my own regiment, conducted me to the marshal's bivouac. The great commander embraced me, thanked me very heartily, and made me share his modest supper, consisting of a cold fowl with a single bottle of wine and a flask of brandy.

During all of next day, the 17th, the two armies confronted each other as if merely on dress parade. In the course of the day an old classmate of mine at school, M. de Coussy, then attached to King Murat as his secretary, came over to the position we maintained on the battlefield, to seek among the dead for a clerk of the prince's staff who had not been heard from since the day before. His search was fruitless, and M. de Coussy, whom I afterwards met in Paris when one of the leading stock brokers of the capital, informed me that this man had never reappeared and that in all probability his disappearance was but a cowardly desertion.

That morning the emperor ordered an intelligent *chasseur* of the escort, who spoke German, to go to the enemy's outposts under cover of a flag of truce and present to Prince Colloredo the compliments of the Prince of Neufchâtel. It was but a stratagem to discover whether this general had joined the enemy's army with the forty thousand Austrians under his command. The *chasseur* only learned that the posts were forbidden to hold any communication

with us, and that he must turn-about-face at once. We spent the
entire day cleaning our arms and equipments and by next day, the
18th, we were, as Major de Vérigny used to say, in the correct style
to be killed.

Nevertheless we spent all this day near a windmill on the plain,
where the emperor's headquarters had been established. The regiment
was held in reserve until evening, and we suffered merely a few losses

from the enemy's heavy guns. I had to deplore the death of one personal friend, a lieutenant of my regiment named Helson, who was struck by a cannonball that ricocheted full against his breast.

At nightfall we made our bivouac behind a hedge. As I was riding toward the spot that had been assigned for my squad, I heard my own name called. It was by one of my friends, a captain in the Guard infantry, who was in company with two other officers of his corps, from their bivouac close by. He invited me to come over to his quarters, as soon as I should he free, and join them in a modest supper.

"I shall do so with pleasure, dear fellow; I'll also bring with me a bottle of brandy which I obtained from a sutler."

A quarter of an hour later, with my loaf of mess-bread and bottle under my arm, I joined Servatius—such was the name of my friend, latterly a colonel of *gendarmes* at Arras. When we were all seated and ready one of the officers emptied into a big tin dish a fragrant stew, made of a hare, chopped into pieces and done brown with plenty of potatoes and onions. The dish was found to be capital. "I see you have found means to send to the Leipzig market," I said to Servatius.

"No, indeed, dear friend," he answered, "but my sergeant-major sent a bullet, not ten yards away from here, through the excellent fat hare we are now despatching, and which was so silly as to cross the battlefield near my famished company."

"But how is it you did not invite the sergeant-major to share with us?"

"Well, there was a little difficulty in the way," replied Servatius, "the sergeant-major had scarcely shot and picked up the hare, and was crying out to me: 'Captain, here is our supper for tonight!' when he was himself hit by a cannonball that sent him to take supper with Pluto. The hare he gave me has turned out to be his legacy, and that is the whole history of our banquet."

"If that is so, my dear Servatius," I observed, handing him the brandy bottle, "I would like to drink the health of that admirable fellow, the late sergeant-major."

We all did so, and soon afterward taking leave of the party I returned to my bivouac, which our regiment again quitted at two o'clock in the morning to re-enter Leipzig. We crossed the bridge over the Elster that was to prove so fatal to our army and to the intrepid Poniatowski.

The stupidity of a corporal in the engineer corps, who had been instructed with four of his men to blow up the bridge as soon as the enemy came in sight, was the immediate cause of this terrible disaster. When a few bullets were fired toward him by Saxon deserters, he instantly set fire to the mine and destroyed the bridge, although we had still on the other side of the river from twenty-two to twenty-five thousand men of the three corps of Reynier, Lauriston and Poinatowski, all slowly retreating, while battling with desperate valour, through the promenades and streets of Leipzig. When those heroes reached the bridge they found nothing left of it but smoking ruins. The first two of these generals were made prisoners. The last, the unfortunate Poniatowski, lost his life in the river, which he attempted to cross, although wounded, by availing himself of his horse's swimming powers. From twenty to twenty-five thousand men were killed, wounded or captured. Among the dead was General Dumoustier of the Imperial Guard.

His Majesty, who slept the night before at the Black Eagle Inn, beyond the Elster bridge, had returned that way at six in the morning,

accompanied by his escort, to the palace of the King of Saxony, to take farewell of the latter, who indeed shed tears at his departure. At seven o'clock the emperor again crossed the ill-fated bridge, followed by the Guard, and was pushing his way along the Erfurth road, when the roar of a tremendous explosion impelled all in the escort to look behind. There we beheld a thick mountain of smoke which at once filled every heart with the presentiment of a great disaster. The emperor immediately turned back, we following him, in the direction of Leipzig. In a brief half hour we knew every detail of the blow that had fallen on our army, I myself being told of it by a man who was inquiring for me all through the regiment, and who had escaped over the river barefoot and naked except for his underclothing. This was my friend M. D'Esclignac, a, captain and *aide-de-camp* of General Raynier, who had managed to elude seizure by swimming through the Elster under a hail of bullets from the Saxon Army. I hastened to fling my cloak over his shoulders and handed him a little flask of brandy, which was a most welcome invigorant.

Our army was then retreating toward Mayence, fighting as it fell

back the one hundred and fifty thousand Austrians who were in pursuit, and later the fifty thousand Bavarians who had now turned enemies and were hurrying toward the fortress of Hanau to cut off our way into France. The troops were still full of spirit and our retreat was in perfect order; the rearguard, under command of the Duke of Trévise, daily repulsed a succession of furious attacks. On October 23rd the regiment of mounted *chasseurs* of the Guard had just reached the Fulda, when we met a train of ambulance wagons tilled with wounded, who were either lying or seated four together in those light vehicles built for the purpose.

"What are you doing here?" I asked Servatius, whom I discovered in one of the wagons.

"My dear Parquin, I am here with three other officers, all of us wounded."

"Are you very badly hurt?"

"I have been hit in the leg by a bullet and am just now suffering torture, for I have not had my wound dressed for three days."

I was suddenly struck with an idea:

"Do you think you can sit in the saddle for a couple of hours?"

"I suppose I could, but I have no horse; both my chargers were left on the wrong side of the Elster bridge."

"Never mind that, I have a horse for you."

I sent at once for my orderly and after a few minutes effort was able to relieve my friend from his very critical position, for even the ambulance would have to be given up after the passage of the Fulda River. I had Servatius' wound dressed by the surgeon-major of my regiment, and afterward was lucky enough to get him to Mayence in fair condition and there place him in the hospital for proper treatment.

I must record here the encounter we had with the Bavarians, who, forty or forty-five thousand strong, were waiting for us at Hanau, on the banks of the Kintzig River. They expected to have an easy task in crushing our retreating army. But it was the Guard, seventeen thousand strong, infantry, cavalry and artillery, with the emperor at its head, that this traitor foe had to deal with!

On the morning of October 30th, Marshal Macdonald was ordered to come out of the woods, but he only succeeded in doing so at noon, so stubborn and so well sustained by formidable artillery was the resistance offered him by the enemy.

A farm to the left of the road, in open country, was vigorously defended by the Bavarians, who had planted themselves in force behind its walls. The emperor summoned General Cambronne. "How many foot *chasseurs* of the Old Guard have you with you?" he asked.

"Eighteen hundred. Sire."

"Then place yourself at their front and carry that farm, which is held by ten thousand Bavarians. I give you two hours to do the job."

It took the intrepid Cambronne just an hour to dislodge the Bavarians. He did not fire a shot, but had simply rushed in, bayonets fixed, and swept like a hurricane the Bavarians who presumed to

meet, even behind improvised ramparts, the assault of the Beehives—
as they called the grenadiers of the Guard because of their huge bear-
skin hats. These veterans of France invariably spread terror wherever
they charged.

Toward three o'clock the whole forest was in possession of our
troops. The artillery had just arrived. General Drout advanced to the
skirt of the woods with fifty cannon of the Guard artillery, planted
them in battery order and opened a destructive fire.

In a movement by fours, which our regiment made along the main
road that crossed the forest, I saw cut down every horse and rider of
the file of four *chasseurs* that immediately preceded me. A single cannonball from the enemy achieved this slaughter. I lifted my horse with
an iron grasp, and digging the spurs deep made him jump over the
ghastly barrier thus suddenly thrown in my way.

The final move of the regiment had for its object the assistance of
our artillery, threatened by Bavarian cavalry. Before we reached the
spot six cannon had been surrounded and the gunners were defending
them with their side-arms, when Captain Oudinot, son of the marshal, charging stoutly with his company of Guard *chasseurs*, recaptured
the guns and saved from certain death the gunners who had been battling against fearful odds.

The grenadiers of the Guard next swept down with tremendous
energy on the Bavarian cavalry. My intrepid friend Guindey, then sub-
adjutant-major in the horse grenadiers—the same officer who had
killed Prince Louis of Prussia at Saalfeld in single combat—was found
dead that evening on the battlefield covered with sabre-cuts, while
nearby were half a dozen dead Bavarian cavalrymen who had thus
atoned for his life.

This officer had heard the emperor, that very morning, say to a
group of cavaliers who had shared his night's bivouac on the skirt of
the forest:

"What do you think of those Bavarians, only yesterday our allies,
who strive to cut off our retreat and hinder us re-entering France
when we are already within sight of the steeples of Mayence?"

"On my honour," cried Guindey, "it is the blackest piece of treachery I ever heard of. But don't you doubt it, Sire, the Bavarians shall pay
dearly for their bravado and their treason."

The success we achieved on the battlefield of Hanau proved how
far right was Guindey's forecast, although he gave up his own life as
part of the cost of victory. I had the privilege of a shake-hands with

him just a moment before he led his charge with the horse grenadiers. He was never to return. Poor Guindey!

It was on this same morning of Hanau that I became acquainted with a son of the illustrious Marshal Moncey. He arrived on a visit to his friend Lauriston, major in the 1st regiment of the Guard of Honour, and Oudinot, captain in the horse *chasseurs* of the Imperial Guard. Major Moncey had just left the infantry, where he served for several

years, to take a commission in the 7th Hussars. He had served all through the Russian campaign as a captain in the foot *chasseurs*. When the emperor was about leaving Smolensk he reviewed his regiment, and after distributing some rewards and crosses to the faithful soldiers, he assembled the officers around him and thus spoke:

"Besides the fortunate ones whose names I have just announced, I have still a cross of the Legion to give to such officer as your corps shall pronounce the most worthy. Your choice shall be mine. Speak out, therefore; for whom do you desire this officer's cross?"

Every voice sounded as one in uttering the name of Moncey.

"Oh, you mean my old page," said the emperor; "I am afraid you are all courtiers and that you offer his name just to please me. Better choose someone else."

"Not so, Sire; we could not choose any name that represents a loftier heroism. Our unanimous verdict is also a sincere one."

"If this he indeed so," replied the emperor, "then here is the officer's cross which I place in your name upon his breast."

In 1818 a hunting accident caused the death of brave Colonel

Moncey, in the flower of his manhood, and just as he seemed to walk in the footsteps of that father whose name is one of the brightest among Frenchmen of high renown.

But let us return to the Battle of Hanau. About four o'clock in the afternoon the 3rd regiment of the Guard of Honour distinguished itself, being its first action on that day, by a superb cavalry charge that initiated the complete rout of the enemy. At five o'clock the battle was ended and we were pushing the Bavarians toward the city of Hanau, their infantry being obliged to recross the Kintzig.

Captain Schmidt, in command of my own squadron of the Guard *chasseurs*, effected the capture of two entire infantry battalions just before the gates of Hanau. It was during this action that I received a bayonet wound in the face.

The enemy lost from six to seven thousand men, killed, wounded or made prisoners. Their general-in-chief, De Wrède, was hit by a bullet that remained in his body until he died, thirty years later.

Next day, the 31st of October, the French Army arrived at Frankfort, and on the 3rd of November entered its own country at Mayence. On the day of the emperor's arrival in this latter city I had the honour of commanding the escort squad in front of the Imperial Palace where he was lodged. When I was relieved from duty, instead of joining my company, which was quartered about three leagues away in one of the suburban villages, I went to the quartermaster of the Imperial Guard and had him distribute to my men the necessary supplies of bread, beer and brandy I then transferred my command to the sergeant of the squad, with orders to bring it back to the cantonment, handing him a few lines, written in pencil, for my captain, whom I thereby informed that I had taken the liberty of remaining a few hours at Mayence, for the purpose of buying several much-needed articles of personal attire. I added that I should report at quarters a little later in the day.

My most urgent need was to get a good square meal, for I had had nothing to eat since the day before, in Frankfort. As I wandered about the city, having the full disposal of my person and time, I approached and entered the first hotel whose sign challenged my gaze. This was the *Pariserhof*, or Hotel of the City of Paris. I found it to contain a crowd of soldiers from every branch of the service, who were filing into the kitchen to broil veal and mutton chops with their own hands. These were the only kinds of meat to be had, and even with these it became necessary to broil one's own chop and to stand by with sabre in hand lest anybody should snatch it away half cooked from the broiler. It was a struggle I soon gave up, having decided to satisfy my hunger with a piece of the ration instead carried by my orderly, all the other hotels and restaurants of Mayence being similarly crowded.

In these circumstances I turned wearily toward the palace gate to proceed to my cantonment, being enabled as I rode through the streets to see from my saddle what was passing on the second floors of most houses. I thus noticed in a room, which was evidently used as a dining hall, a table having the service laid for ten people. It was just as a domestic was closing the window-shutters that I made this valuable discovery. My hunger suggested an idea which I at once put into execution. Dismounting in front of the house I gave my horse in charge of my orderly. I skipped up the outside steps and began hammering with the knocker. A man servant came to the door and asked me in German:

"What is it you wish, sir?"

"I want to speak to your master."

"Ah, you wish to see Herr Hosemann," he replied, and led me at once into the dining-room.

There he handed me a seat and went out to notify his master of the presence of a visitor.

"Monsieur Hosemann," I said to a gentlemen who now approached me, and whom I assumed to be the master of the house, "will you have the extreme kindness to ask, in my behalf, the mistress of this house to give me a seat at her table? It is over two hours since I crossed the Mayence bridge escorting the emperor; I have not eaten anything for twenty-four hours and I find it impossible to procure decent food in this city, crowded as it is with troops and famished visitors. As I passed your door a few minutes ago I noticed the well-arranged table, and I thought that perhaps the lady and gentleman of the house would take pity on my condition. If I have made a mistake, sir, I am ready to retire."

"Mr. Officer, my wife here present," replied M. Hosemann, presenting me to one of the ladies who had now entered the room, "does not speak French; but knowing her kindly heart I have no doubt she will be pleased to have you sit at her table. We have also here some friends whom we have invited to dinner."

I thanked him, bowed to the assembled ladies and gentlemen, and was at once assigned to a seat next Madame Hosemann, on whom I began exploiting the little German I could speak. Her husband was the only one in the company who knew our language. I understood

that he held a high office in the forestry department. As the conversation took place in German I had no share in it, but I did justice to a dinner that was truly excellent. Having begged M. Hosemann to send one of his servants with a bottle of wine to my orderly, who was holding my horse in the street, the master of the house directed that the brave fellow should be invited into the courtyard, and our two horses be stabled. The *chasseur* was then conducted to the kitchen

and enjoyed just as good a meal as his officer—in a word, M. Hose-mann proved himself a most generous caterer. Four o'clock sounded from the cathedral steeple. When the company had concluded dinner and were chatting over their coffee I took my leave, but not without warmly thanking them for their kind hospitality. As I handed my card to M. Hosemann, I pleasantly observed:

"Usually, sir, I call for the bill after dinner; here I shall only present you with this little souvenir, which may remind you in future days of the officer in the Imperial Guard whom you treated with such benevolence. For my part I shall gratefully cherish your name and that of your excellent lady."

In departing I gave a *thaler* to the servant who had presented my name to his master when I entered the house; then I mounted my horse and set out for the cantonment, which I reached at seven o'clock.

We spent our time in this bivouac furbishing up the arms and uniforms. After so rapid and disastrous a campaign they were in great need of such attention. The concentration around Mayence of such a large number of troops, whose wounded and sick crowded every hospital, soon gave rise to an epidemic of typhus that carried off, in a few days, hundreds of brave fellows whom death had spared on many a battlefield. The village where we passed the week was rather an important borough, on which had been levied a heavy war tribute, and its inhabitants were compelled besides to furnish all kinds of supplies to the Mayence garrison.

On the eve of our departure I was seated by the fireplace in the kitchen of my host, who was one of the prominent citizens of the place. He himself stood close to his open door, and was narrating with much spirit to a neighbour what befell him that morning at Mayence, whither he had been with a wagonload of hay. My orderly, who was in the room, understood German and interpreted for me the leading points of the story. Here they are:

The mortality had grown so frightfully since the invasion of typhus that all country wagons bringing military supplies to Mayence were requisitioned by the authorities immediately after their loads were examined, accepted, and stored. The vehicles were then employed to carry to the cemetery the dead that were accumulating in the hospitals. This gruesome work was only done at night. My host narrated that when his load had been accepted by the quartermaster, his own wagon and team of four stout horses were impressed into the service described. He had made one trip from the hospital to the graveyard and was starting again with the second load. While passing the city gate that led out to his village, he whipped up one of the foremost horses so angrily that it took fright and suddenly veered to the left, swinging off the other horses on a gallop. The team and its driver were soon far out of the city. My host then bethought himself of a scheme for getting rid of his load. Every five minutes or so he loosened a trap-board at the bottom of his wagon and thus allowed one of the cadavers to drop on the load, so that by the time he reached the village he had but a single corpse left. This he brought over to the churchyard with the remark that it certainly deserved Christian burial. I could not help thinking to myself that this stolid-looking German was fully as sharp as many of our Norman farmers who are reputed to be so tricky in their dealings.

The emperor, after spending five days at Mayence in reorganising the army, left that city on the 6th of November for Paris, arriving home at Saint-Cloud on the 9th. On the 1st of December we broke up our cantonments to march into the interior of France. On the 21st, while cantoned in Champagne, I received my brevet as captain in the 2nd regiment of Guard *chasseurs*. Though delighted at the promotion I regretted leaving my company, particularly on account of Captain Klein de Kleinberg, who had shown me great kindness. The paymaster of the regiment, M. Brice, as he handed me my brevet, also gave me a written order from General Lefèbvre-Desnouettes to join him at Paris, to take command of the 11th company of horse *chasseurs*, an organization that had been formed out of the non-commissioned officers of the Old Guard. Paymaster Brice further intrusted to me twenty bags of one thousand *francs* each, to be handed over to one Rabusson, the military tailor who had the contract for clothing the regiment. This money and its responsibility worried me and interfered very much with my proper rest. Having reached Saint-Dizier by post-chaise I there found General Cambronne, whom I had the honour of knowing and whom I found to be worried himself by the fact that he had in his possession a number of ten-day treasury-drafts for the pay of his regiment. I proposed to exchange with him the twenty thousand *francs* in specie which I carried for the twenty thousand *francs* of treasury paper, thus rendering him as well as myself a substantial service. General Cambronne thanked me most kindly and gave me a choice dinner at Saint-Dizier.

I arrived at Paris on December 23rd, having taken post-horses from Saint-Dizier in fellowship with a colonel of cavalry and a captain of the horse grenadiers of the Guard. All three of us had been promoted and had to take this journey in consequence. At the end of the campaign in France, I was the only survivor of the three. The colonel lost his life in the Battle of Montmirail, and the captain at the battle of Craonne.

On the 1st day of January 1814, I was home again with my family. Eleven years before, in the same month and on the same day, I had en-

305

listed as a volunteer. I had since risen on the battlefield to be a captain in the horse *chasseurs* of the Guard, and a member of the Legion of Honour. My parents, indeed, had reasonable cause to be proud of me, for I was still only twenty-six years of age, yet they never gave me to understand that they were so but constantly showed themselves averse to my warlike proclivities.

I duly took command as captain of the 11th company, and had to

leave on the 9th of February to join the Old Guard in Champagne, the rest of my regiment being still in the Army of the North before Antwerp. I do not understand to this day how I was so lucky as to pass safely through the entire French campaign, side by side with the Old Guard *chasseurs* and a company of the emperor's own Mamelukes. The captain of the Mamelukes rode beside me. He happened to be considerably my senior as captain, for his promotion dated from the formation of his corps under the Consulate. But a special regulation in the Guard provided that all foreigners, Egyptians, Poles, Italians or Hollanders, whatever their precedence might be on the army list, were to yield the command of a detachment to any native French officer of similar rank. The captain I speak of had been on the retired list already for fourteen years and lived in the city of Marseilles. Later he had rejoined the Mamelukes in obedience to a decree of the emperor, promulgated after the invasion of France by the Allies, which may be said to date from the 2nd of January, 1814.

Captain Ibrahim-Bey was in command of the company of Mamelukes that came to France after the Egyptian campaign. On the day of his first arrival in Paris he lost his way. His oriental costume interested the Parisians, and curiosity soon gathered a considerable crowd after him. In the public market he was surrounded by a lot of loafers who jeered and hooted him, threw mud over his clothes and shouted that this was no carnival time to be promenading in fancy costume. Captain Ibrahim-Bey did not understand French, but neither did he tolerate insult, and so he drew his pistols and in an instant had shot dead two of the most stalwart market porters. Then swinging his scimitar round his head with one hand and brandishing his dagger in the other, he would certainly have slain some more had not the patrol come along and over powered him after considerable trouble. The occur-

rence was duly narrated to the First Consul, General Bonaparte, who at once sent for Ibrahim-Bey. The latter stated fearlessly that he had acted only as he had always done in Egypt when the rabble presumed to insult a Mameluke.

"You are not here to play policeman," retorted the First Consul, through an interpreter. "Tomorrow you shall start for Marseilles; there you will find a warmer climate, and I shall see that you are paid regularly a six thousand *franc* pension, less two thousand *francs* which

will be handed over to the two widows made by your own hands. At Marseilles people don't stare when they see a Turk or Arab in his national costume, but I forbid you to use or even carry your weapons about with you."

Submitting himself to these orders Captain Ibrahim-Bey never touched his weapons again until he was called, fourteen years later, to bear arms against the invaders of France.

On the 6th of February, 1814, our detachment of the Guard Cavalry, six hundred strong, set out from Paris under command of Major Kirmann, my former captain in the 20th Chasseurs, to join the army. We reached the staff headquarters on the 10th, the eve of the Battle of Montmirail. On the 11th, at noon, being then in the field, I received from General Colbert the order to charge with my company on the left of a Russian square which was also assailed on the right by General Letort and a squadron of Guard dragoons. Our double charge succeeded to perfection, both squadrons meeting in the centre of the Russian square.

The Russians felt so sure of being able to repel our attack that they had ranged their knapsacks along the ground. When we took this square we made our prisoners pick them up and drop their guns on the soil instead.

The farm of Gréneaux was the most difficult position to carry, being defended by a formidable array of artillery. The enemy were barricaded up to their chins behind the farm walls, and we failed to dislodge them until about two o'clock in the afternoon. The emperor had intrusted Marshal Ney with this difficult task. The marshal dismounted and sword in hand, placed himself at the head of six battalions of the Guard. Before rushing forward he ordered his men to throw away the primings of their guns. His purpose was to strike the enemy at the point of the bayonet only, and so gallantly did he lead the charge that his audacity proved entirely successful. The Russians and Prussians retreated from the farm, abandoning all their cannon, ammunition-wagons, and even their canteens.

Just as Marshal Ney had thus settled the day's victory, General Baron Henrion received orders to send his regiments of foot *chasseurs* of the Guard to capture a redoubt, filled with the enemy's artillery, and on which a brigade of our infantry had failed to produce an impression. Baron Henrion formed his attacking column and pushed it forward on the double-quick, so as not to allow any pause under the terrible fire of the enemy. General Sacken at once apprehended the danger to his cannon if the attacking column should reach them, and to baffle

the French infantry threw upon its right wing a strong force of cavalry. Seeing this manoeuvre, General Henrion commanded at once:

"Column—Halt! Form square! Present—Ready—Fire!"

The cavalry column, which was not over ten feet away, was almost decimated by the close fusillade and had to turn back in disorder, leaving on the ground a number of dead and wounded. Without losing a moment General Henrion resumed his advance, and, not even giving his *chasseurs* time to reload their guns, pushed on toward the redoubt. He captured it, too, in spite of the desperate resistance of the Russian artillerymen, who suffered themselves to be impaled against their cannon rather than surrender.

The emperor, who followed this movement attentively, galloped over to the captured redoubt, and said to General Henrion, while shaking him by the hand, and naming him a commander in the Legion of Honour:

"General, I fully approve of that pause in your charge."

The carrying of this redoubt and of the Gréneaux farm decided the fate of the day. The victory was complete.

The Prussian corps of General York and the Russians under General Sacken effected their retreat, or to speak more accurately, their flight, in the direction of Château-Thierry. We overtook their column on the 14th, about a league from the place named. One of my old chiefs in the 20th Chasseurs, Colonel Curély then in command of the 10th Hussars, gained his promotion here to brigadier-general as the reward for two brilliant charges which he made at the head of his regiment. He had the Prussians against him and the eyes of the emperor watching his success. On the day after the Battle of Montmirail the enemy had neither artillery, baggage, nor wagons, having even abandoned their wounded to the generosity of the victors and scampered into Château-Thierry to place the river Marne between them and our army.

Satisfied that these two divisions were now completely routed, the emperor, by a brilliant movement, directed his whole Guard against Prince Schwartzenberg's army, which was advancing along the banks of the Seine. He caught up with it in the plain of Nangis on the 17th. Our dragoons, who had just returned from Spain under command of General Treilhard, inflicted on the Austrians a total defeat, and one which would have placed their entire army in our power if Marshal Victor had carried out the emperor's order to seize on the Montereau bridge.

On the 2nd of March the main portion of the Prussian Army, under command of Marshal Blucher and accompanied by a Russian army corps, crossed the river Marne at Château-Thierry. The Prussians were in such haste to escape from us, hotly pursued as they were by the emperor, that they destroyed a section of the Marne bridge to obstruct our advance. This had the result of securing for them a comparatively safe retreat, while it imposed on us a delay of twenty-four hours which proved a much-needed rest. The emperor established his headquarters in the postmaster's house of the suburb where we had been in position. On the arrival of the engineer corps next day His Majesty came down to the river bank as early as ten o'clock to assure himself that the bridge was put again into serviceable condition. His Majesty asked General Bertrand, his Grand Marshal, who was superintending the work, how many hours would he needed to complete it. General Bertrand replied that he would have it finished in four hours.

"I shall give you six," observed the emperor.

And at four o'clock in the afternoon the bridge was again in condition for transit. General Colbert, who commanded the Guard brigade to which I belonged, had ordered me the same morning to hold myself in readiness with one hundred cavalry of the Old Guard to carry out a mission of which I should learn during the day from the emperor's own lips. About four o'clock I rode at the head of my squadron toward the bridge and presented myself to the emperor. His Majesty said to me:

"Captain, push on after the enemy at full speed and bring me back a few prisoners, I need them."

Knowing that three roads started from Château-Thierry, leading respectively to Soissons, La Ferté' and Reims, I asked him:

"What road must I take, Sire?"

"The Soissons highway," he answered.

Such a flattering confidential mission received from such a source was sure to lead to admirable results. I marched my squadron over the bridge by fours, letting the horses walk. When we reached the further bank I allowed my men to accept, without retarding their pace, the bread, cognac, ham and other edibles which the citizens of Château-Thierry plentifully gave them, so happy were these worthy people to see French soldiers again, after having lodged Russians and Prussians whose conduct in their peaceful community was little short of barbarous.

I passed away from Château-Thierry and the loyal enthusiasm of its citizens, and had ridden about three leagues farther on the Soissons road, when the march of my squadron was interrupted by the

flames that were consuming a deserted hamlet. The inhabitants, rather than endure the brutality of the invader, had preferred, even in mid-winter, to seek shelter in the neighbouring woods. I had vainly caused the place to be searched to discover any living soul, so as to pick up information about the route of Generals Sacken and Blucher, when a sergeant in the Guard *chasseurs*, one of my search party, came back with a report that in the last house of the hamlet—the only one still untouched by the flames—he had espied a party of stragglers from the Prussian Army, stretched round the kitchen fire and apparently waiting for their food to be cooked. The sergeant added that a few *chasseurs* of my squadron would be quite enough to capture this gang of foot soldiers. He managed the raid himself very cleverly. He ordered the *chasseurs* that accompanied him to level their loaded carbines against the windowpanes of the house, pointing the muzzles in the direction of the fireplace, where the unsuspecting Prussians were seated. One may imagine how frightened the latter were, when, in obedience to the sergeant's command the bullets began to whiz about their ears. Next the sergeant rushed with drawn sabre into the house, with his *chasseurs* close behind, and made captive all the men inside, none of whom had been wounded. He at once led them back to the front of my troop, which had been kept waiting at the other end of the village.

If France were not at the time under invasion by the allied armies, I should have been greatly amused at our capture of a monster caldron in which over thirty fowls were cooking, besides hams, potatoes, etc. We also found in the room a quantity of bread cut up for immediate distribution, all forming a most savoury supper and one which my *chasseurs* enjoyed immensely.

Under the strict laws of war and considering the exceptional position I was in with my little squadron, I had the right to immediately order the shooting of these Russian grenadiers of General Sacken's army, surprised as they had been in a village burned down by the enemy. But in ordering me to bring hack some prisoners the emperor had unwittingly saved their lives. I decided, therefore, to practice a

little generosity and to invite them to the supper they had themselves prepared, and which had caused their capture, inasmuch as it was only their eagerness to enjoy the good things of the village that had tempted them to straggle behind the main body of the army. They had doubtless intended to recover lost time by a forced night march. The sudden arrival of my troop had simply frustrated their plans.

The information I gathered from these prisoners convinced me I was on the right track and that the enemy was hurriedly retreating in the direction of Soissons.

After this brief halt I proceeded on my way, leaving the prisoners with my rearguard under the personal supervision of the sergeant who commanded it. When we had gone about a league farther, it being now past nightfall, my scouts informed me that the enemy was occupying the large village of Oulchy-le-Château, four leagues from Soissons. I hastened to notify General Colbert, whom I knew to be marching behind me with a brigade of Guard cavalry, that the rearguard of the enemy had posted its sentries this side of Oulchy-le-Château and that the village was fully occupied, the numerous tires of the bivouacs denoting the presence of a strong force. I also notified him that I was about to carry into execution the order I had received from the emperor and begged him to support my movement with a few squadrons of cavalry, as it was most probable that the enemy on recovering from their first surprise would try to punish me as much as possible in my retreat.

Having taken these precautions I also gave my men and horses a little time to cool off and get a drink, and then started the squadron at a walking pace along the grassy margin of the road. Soon I discovered the enemy about a hundred yards ahead, and at once heard the guttural *Wer da?* (Who goes there?) of the sentry. Then I struck my men into a gallop and quickly captured the sentinel, the relieving watch and the main guard, every one of whom we completely surprised. Crossing Oulchy-le-Château I next galloped my squadron into the Russian and Prussian bivouacs, everywhere spreading confusion and dismay. The sleepers only awoke to find themselves sabred or pierced through by my *chasseurs* and lancers, or else stricken down by the fire of dragoons and Mamelukes, whose weapons included pistols and carbines. My squadron had been purposely made up of these various elements of the Old Guard cavalry.

Being surprised in this audacious manner in the middle of the night, of course the enemy thought themselves attacked by at least

several cavalry regiments. The confusion we created was indescribable. We left behind us a number of killed and wounded and I captured altogether about one hundred prisoners, among whom were two colonels and several subalterns. All these were conducted immediately to the emperor, who was then at Fismes.

His Majesty learned from them that General Moreau, who commanded the fortress of Soissons, had opened its gates to the Allies in response to their very first summons.

"That name ever brings me disaster," was Napoleon's observation when he heard the name of Moreau.

In the bold and successful raid accomplished by my squadron, M. Pellion, who led the party that attacked the Russian rearguard, shot down with his own hand the officer who commanded it. As this single feat had greatly contributed to the success of our enterprise, I was glad to mention the fact and to eulogize heartily M. Pellion's dash and intrepidity. At present this gentlemen is a colonel on the general staff and attached to the Minister of War.

The position of the enemy would have been most critical if it were not for their admission within the gates of the city of Soissons. The road from Château-Thierry to Laferté was covered by Marshal Macdonald, at the head of an army corps of seventeen thousand men. The Reims highway had no road-bed and was therefore impracticable for marching troops during this season of the year. The enemy was accordingly crowded against Soissons, and the emperor, Marshal Mortier and the Guard were all there to force a surrender. But fate, alas! was declaring against us.

On the 5th of March General Colbert sent me to reconnoitre along the Fismes road. The officer commanding the advance pursued a few Cossack scouts, and imprudently pushed with his squad into the narrow defile between the Quincampoix mills. On hastening to his assistance with the three other troops of my squadron, I soon discovered that I had to meet much larger forces than I at first suspected. Moreover, as I had been sent forward simply to reconnoitre and not to fight the enemy, I ordered a retreat. In making this movement it was necessary to walk our horses. This gave the enemy an opportunity to surround us, and even to cut off our retreat by the Soissons road. I had therefore to sabre my way through about five hundred Cossacks, of the Russian army corps commanded by General Wintzingerode. This general was himself hard pressed by General Nansouty, who, at the head of the Guard cavalry, gained a victory over him at Berry-Au-Bac. To cut my way through this swarm of cavalry I had to submit to heavy losses. In fact, two of my offic-

ers were wounded and captured, M. De Montalembert, son of the speaker of the Chamber of Deputies, and M. Lacrosse, a son of the admiral of that name, and today a member of the legislature. Nearly fifty *chasseurs* of my squadron were killed, wounded or captured. I myself received a lance-wound in the arm. My reconnaissance, however, rendered an important service to the army, which otherwise would have been surprised from the rear. When I returned from my mission and reported to General Colbert, he simply observed, alluding to the brilliant picnic to which I treated the enemy at Oulchy-le-Château on that memorable night in March:

"One cannot be always lucky in war."

"You are right, general," said I, "but at least I have the satisfaction to assure you that my officers and soldiers used their sabres lustily The proof of it is that half of my squadron is disabled, and as for myself, I must ask your kind permission to go over to the ambulance and have this lance-wound in my left arm properly treated."

Happily the wound proved of little importance; it did not even hinder me from taking part in the campaign. When France was invaded all her children had to defend her, and I, as one of them, was too proud to think of being absent from my post. Some cologne and lint, with a little bathing, my favourite applications, soon remedied this trifling mishap.

Two days later, on the 7th of March, took place the Battle of Craonne. Generals Nansouty and Grouchy, in command of the Guard cavalry, obtained a great success in several charges that took place upon the plateau. Both these commanders were wounded, and General Laferrière, major of the horse grenadiers of the Guard, had a foot smashed by a cannonball, a condition which necessitated the amputation of the leg. He submitted to the operation with unflinching courage, crying out repeatedly: "Long live the Emperor!" My friend Captain Achintre, of the 1st regiment of Guard Chasseurs, was cut down by a cannonball; he had announced that very morning that this would be his last day on earth. At two o'clock his prediction was realized. He was an old officer who had belonged to the Egyptian Guides, and his entire regiment mourned him deeply.

With my squadron I was kept constantly under the fire of the enemy's artillery. Lieutenant Numance de Girardin had the scabbard of his sabre shattered and his horse killed by a ball. He attributed his narrow escape to a sword-knot given him by a very pretty Parisian, Madame Lavollée. It was a talisman, he used to say, that warded off all danger from his person. The same evening in bivouac I told this young officer—who was going through his first campaign—how it often happened that a cannonball which comes very close to you without actually striking, would cause internal injury if the body on that side were not diligently rubbed with some good brandy. To obtain this preventive he found it necessary to send about a league's distance to a neighbouring town. A peasant who was lounging at our bivouac fire was intrusted with the mission, and was given a gold *napoleon* to pay for the fire-water and for his trouble. He returned two hours later with four bottles of brandy. This class of supply was quite scarce at the time and rather expensive; even the sutlers were very short of it. M. de Girardin was then sleeping such a sound and

refreshing nap that it would have been positive cruelty to wake him up. Our real object was to have him pay his footing among us; for of course he ran no danger on account of the cannonball mentioned. When he woke up in the morning he took the joke in excellent humour and together we drank our, or rather *his* brandy, to the health of the Parisian lady who had given him his talisman.

I no longer remember the trifling incident which brought about a quarrel between Captain Ibrahim-Bey and Captain Lindsay, *aide-de-camp* of General Lefébvre-Desnouettes. Anyhow it resulted in the two gentlemen named deciding to step apart behind the wall of a neighbouring farm and settle their dispute with swords, I did my best to reason with Ibrahim-Bey, who had entreated me to be his second.

I insisted that a duel between officers was a bad example, and that France being invaded, the life of every one of her sons, her defenders, belonged exclusively to her. Captain Lindsay understood me thoroughly, but the Mameluke only repeated, in his broken language, half French, half Arabic: "Now see, comrade, when I am friend I am gentle, very gentle, and affectionate as a little dog; but when I am angry I

must have battle; I am a true lion." And as he uttered these last words Ibahim's eyes seemed to start out of his head.

"Well, if it is so, be friends and shake hands, don't you see that Captain Lindsay is offering you his hand?"

This appeal had its effect on the captain of the Mamelukes, for he yielded. A few days later, Ibrahim-Bey, being in command of the skirmishers in the plain, was fighting like a veritable lion of the Sahara. During this service his turban became disarranged and its folds blinded him, when he was overtaken by the Cossacks and disabled and captured after he had slain or wounded half a dozen of his adversaries.

Having turned the fortress of Soissons, which was occupied by Sacken, Blucher and Wintzingerode, we arrived on the 9th at Laon. That night my squadron was on vanguard duty in front of a position occupied by the enemy, so I went over to the main post to locate the videttes; and relieving guard, a duty that in actual campaign I always performed myself. In returning I met a corporal of my squadron carrying a bundle of hay on his head, in despite of the strict orders I had given that none of my troop should dismount until I returned. The corporal, whom I reprimanded rather sternly, dropped his bundle at once, but I was so exasperated to see my orders disobeyed under such circumstances, that I struck the delinquent with the flat of the unsheathed sabre I had in my hand. With a sudden movement the poor fellow bared his breast, and displaying his cross of the Legion that shimmered in the moonlight, placed his hand upon his sabre hilt, and said to me.

"Captain, for twenty-two faithful years I have been serving my country and my emperor; for two years I have been a member of the Legion of Honour, and in this one moment you have dishonoured me forever."

I was so mortified to have thus allowed myself to grievously insult a veteran that I hastened to reply:

"Listen, corporal. If I were of your own rank, I wouldn't hesitate to grant you satisfaction, for I am not afraid of you; but I am your captain, and the only thing I can do is to apologize. I now do so; will you shake hands with me:'"

"With pleasure, captain. The whole matter is forgotten," replied the corporal, pressing my hand cordially. Then he picked up his bunch of hay and re-entered the bivouac.

Half an hour later he shared my modest supper, and we drank together a goblet of the remaining brandy.

Next day, which was the 10th, while under fire from the enemy, a cannonball reached a file of Guard *chasseurs* ranged in front of my squadron, and knocked down two men. Since the Battle of Hanau I had not witnessed such bloodshed caused by one projectile. On the 13th we countermarched towards Reims. General Corbineau had been obliged to abandon this city. General Philippe de Ségur, at the head of his regiment of the Guard of Honour, now re-entered the place and dashed pell-mell upon the Russians, whom he drove out at the point of the sabre. General de Saint-Priest, who commanded the Russians, was a French "emigrant" and perished in the fight. A fragment of a shell wounded the horse I was riding. It was the excellent steed that I brought with me from Spain, and which had belonged to the English officer I struck down.

"Captain, we have just taken another horse from the enemy for you," spoke out one of my *chasseurs*.

"All right," I replied, thanking him; "but I doubt very much whether any horse we may capture will ever equal the one I have lost and to which I was so much attached."

On the 19th the emperor marched toward the enemy at La Ferté; on the 20th, we reached Arcis-sur-Aube. It was there that a shell, falling close to the horse he was riding, exploded and covered him with

grime His Majesty, who noticed that this accident had somewhat disturbed a square of the Guard infantry, formed up at a short distance from him, cried out "Have no fear, my children; the shell that is to kill me has not yet been cast."

On the 20th of March, after a short stay at Saint-Dizier, we had resumed the advance toward Vassy, when the loud booming of a cannonade was heard in our rear. Marshal Oudinot's corps, which was to relieve ours at Saint-Dizier, was the object of a vigorous attack by the Russian Army. As soon as this news was brought to the emperor, by one of the marshal's *aides-de-camp*, His Majesty diverted the route of the Guard cavalry, crossed the river Marne at the ford near Valcourt, and by a skilful manoeuvre soon placed us on the right flank of the Russians.

I was riding with my command at the head of the column when the general approached and ordered me to charge at full gallop against three batteries of eighteen cannon which the Russians had established in the open plain. Instantly I complied with the order, but by the time we were about a hundred paces from the cannon their showers of grape-shot had so mercilessly thinned my squadron that I commanded a deploy of two platoons to the right and two to the left, in skirmishing order, thus leaving the middle plain unoccupied. The Red Lancers of the Guard immediately swept into the opening and also charged the enemy's cannon; we captured every one of them.

A division of Russian *cuirassiers* having come to the help of their artillery, collided with the Guard lancers, but these being promptly assisted by the 3rd and 6th Dragoons, under command of General Milland, speedily routed this ponderous cavalry and took about six hundred prisoners. In this affray I unhorsed, by a sabre-thrust that reached his neck, a stalwart sergeant of the Russian *cuirassiers*. A *chasseur* of my squadron straightway grabbed at the horse of the defeated Russian, exclaiming to me: "You have not been long securing a new mount, captain."

"I am pleased to say I have not," I answered, "but give the prisoner his saddlebags: I have been a captive myself in Russia, and I know how much a soldier suffers when he is deprived of all his traps."

The whipping we gave the Russians was thorough. Even their infantry, which was retreating by forced marches on the road to Bar-sur-Ornain, would have been seriously endangered were it not that the approach of night and the nearness of the forest alike served to shield them. The emperor himself, at the head of the Guard cavalry, was leading the pursuit.

The first result of this grand day's fighting was that the Duke of Reggio was enabled to enter Saint-Dizier.

It was the last time the Guard drew its steel against the enemy. But the occasion was not unworthy of closing this splendid campaign of 1814, which tacticians have often compared, so far as manoeuvring was concerned, to General Bonaparte's famous Italian campaigns.

In the report which General Sebastiani presented that evening to the emperor, he expressed himself as follows:

"Sire! I have been for twenty years a cavalry officer, but have never before witnessed a more brilliant charge than that which was executed today by your vanguard squadron."

These flattering words were repeated to me and were indeed very pleasing to the squadron, and to myself as its commander; but still I should have preferred receiving the officer's cross of the Legion of Honour. Major Kirmann, under whose immediate orders I was placed during this campaign, informed me that he had asked the decoration for me after my lucky affair of the 2nd of March.

On the evening of the 26th, when in bivouac, I was delighted to find that the horse I had captured was a first-class animal, and once more agreeably surprised when I discovered a flask of champagne secreted in one of the holsters. My first pleasant notion was to open the bottle and share it with the *chasseur*, whom I soon found to have been the purveyor of it. I again felt deeply mortified, however, as I reflected that the Russians were trampling over this, our own province of Champagne. Whither were the days fled in which we dated our bulletins from Vienna, from Dresden, from Berlin, from Madrid, from Moscow, from Lisbon——?

About the 27th of March, when in bivouac before Saint-Dizier, the emperor was notified of a patriotic uprising that seemed impending among the people of the Vosges in Alsace and Lorraine. He thereupon decided to send Captain Brice, of the 1st regiment of Guard Chasseurs, on the perilous mission of passing through the enemy's forces to reach the Vosges country, of which he was a native, for the purpose of bringing about a general armament of the population. This officer was one of the bravest in the army and proved on the occasion that he deserved the emperor's confidence. Disguised as a teamster he made his way through the whole force of the enemy that lay between him and his compatriots.

On the 28th, at the head of the Guard, the emperor marched toward Troyes and crossed the village of Brienne. A short distance from

this place is the town of Brienne-la-Ville, where one of my relatives
was pastor of the principal church. Desiring greatly to call upon him
I rode ahead of the column so as to spend a few hours in his society.
When I reached the village I asked a peasant girl, whom I met coming
out of the church with a prayer-book in her hand, whether she could
point me out the dwelling of his reverence Vicar Goffrin.

"Alas, my dear sir," she replied in a sorrowful tone, "the worthy
vicar died yesterday and his funeral is now taking place. And truly he

has gone to Paradise, if anybody is rightly rewarded for all the good he did in this world."

"Why my good girl." I exclaimed, "how did it happen that the vicar died so suddenly?"

"Well,. indeed, *Monsieur*, that has been a surprise to us all, for in despite of his seventy-six years he was as hale and hearty as a man of fifty. Nevertheless he fell dead yesterday as he was walking from the church to his house."

I understood by later inquiry that my good kinsman had been struck down in an apoplectic seizure. Having no further object in the village I merely waited for the column and joined my squadron. Next day I obtained twenty-four hours' furlough that I might precede the regiment into Troyes. Accompanied by my orderly I entered this place on the 29th, and at once proceeded to discover the dwelling of M. Couturier, a leading business man and an intimate friend of my brother, the barrister. My orderly knocked at the gate and asked if M. Couturier was at home.

"Yes, sir, he is," answered one of the servant maids, who was weeping bitterly, "but he died this morning and has not yet been buried."

I immediately turned away and rode toward an inn, the Post Hotel, where I hailed with satisfaction the jovial face of its proprietor, who supplied me very willingly, for cash down, with all that was required for my orderly, myself and our horses.

On the following day the emperor left Troyes with one thousand cavalry of his Guard, whose horses were fresh enough for a, prolonged and rapid ride. My own steed and myself had enjoyed such a, good rest at the Post Hotel that I joined the expedition. We travelled along the road to Fontainebleau, where we arrived at noon on the 31st. We had ridden the twenty-five leagues in twenty-seven hours. From Fontainebleau the emperor took post-horses to reach Paris, there to take personal command of the army corps of Marshals Marmont and Mortier, while awaiting the arrival of the force that was marching by stages from Troyes to the capital. He was informed at Villejuif, however, by General Belliard, of the capitulation of the two marshals. At once His Majesty returned to Fontainebleau and took up his residence in the Imperial Palace.

In the meantime the army was pursuing its march from Troyes to Fontainebleau, and speedily the entire Guard was bivouacking in its famous forest. On the 1st and 2nd of April sinister rumours began to float around. On the 3rd, after a review of the troops by the emperor, the following order of the day was read to every company.

"Soldiers! The enemy have stolen three days' march upon us, and are now in possession of Paris. They must he driven out of it. Un-worthy Frenchmen, most of them 'emigrants' whom we had par-doned, have raised the white cockade and joined our enemy. The cowards! They shall be fitly punished for this new treason. Let us swear to vanquish or die, and to fight until we have compelled them

all to respect this tricolour which we have borne for twenty years along the path of honour!"

From all sides came the shouts: "Long live the Emperor! On to Paris!" Our hearts were still beating with valour and hope.

The emperor then had at Fontainebleau some fifty thousand men, twenty-five thousand of whom, including a numerous artillery, belonged to the Guard. there were also the army corps of Marshals Marmont and Mortier and of General Souhan, and the cavalry division of General

Belliard. Having control of both banks of the Seine, His Majesty could have reached Charenton at the head of one hundred thousand men. The brave Parisian population would most certainly have furnished fifty thousand volunteers who could have joined the emperor two leagues from the capital. At that moment the enemy's strength was not over one hundred and thirty thousand, of which at least thirty thousand would be required to stay behind in Paris. Besides, the invaders who had flocked toward Paris in defiance of all prudence, were without ammunition, artillery and baggage. Their retreat toward the Rhine was practically cut off. The allied sovereigns were therefore compelled either to sign the peace in Paris itself, or to effect an escape toward the sea-coast, where they might embark their troops upon the English fleet that was cruising in the channel. Such was their alternative; only treachery in our own ranks could extricate them from this unpleasant dilemma.

On the 9th of April an order of the day from the emperor was addressed to the army, branding as infamous the conduct of the Duke of Ragusa and the Senate, and stating that His Majesty had sent to Paris the Prince of Moskowa, the Duke of Vicenza and the Duke of Tarentum to enter into negotiations. This filled the hearts of the soldiers with grief and indignation.

The 11th of April was the date of Napoleon's abdication, and on the 20th of the same month, at noon, the emperor bade farewell to his assembled Guard. These were the words he uttered and which will forever echo in the soul of every veteran of the Empire:

"Officers, non-commissioned officers, and soldiers of my Old Guard: I now bid you *adieu*. For twenty years we have been together

and I was pleased with you. I always found you on the path to glory. All the powers of Europe have leagued in arms against me. A few of my generals have betrayed their duty, and France herself has wished for another destiny. With you and the other heroes who have continued faithful to me, I might have maintained a civil war. But France would have been made unhappy. Be faithful to your new Sovereign;

obey your new leaders; do not forsake our beloved country: do not pity my fate—I shall be happy as long I know that you are happy yourselves. It is my own wish to die: if I consent to survive, it is to add something more to your fame. I shall put into writing all the great deeds we have done together. I cannot embrace you all, but I will embrace your general. Come, General Petit, let me press you upon my heart. Bring me your eagle, that I may kiss it also. Ah, dear eagle! May the kisses I give to thee resound through all posterity. *Adieu*, my children. My prayer shall accompany you everywhere; may you also keep me in remembrance!"

What floods of tears did these words cause to flow! They were addressed to true veterans—to men who admired while they wept over the huge abnegation. By a spontaneous and unanimous accord, as soon as their emperor had left them, his soldiers burned the eagles, and it is even said that a few, not to be parted from them, swallowed down the ashes.

On the same day the emperor left Fontainebleau, taking with him the Grand Marshal of the Palace, and drove along the Lyons road, where he was attended by the commissioners of the allies and preceded by the battalion of his Guard that was to accompany him to the island of Elba.

Thus ended, in 1814, the marvellous epoch of the Empire which began in 1804.

A Russian diplomat, M. de Nesselrode, once said, in speaking of it:

"What remains now of that great political drama? A Gascon in the North and a Gascon in the South." He was referring to Murat and to Bernadotte. Yes, indeed, what does remain of this great political drama? The vast majority would say, and perhaps M. de Nesselrode himself, were he to answer the question seriously, that if the extraordinary man who presided over these great times went down in the conflict, all the

results he aimed at did not vanish with him. Assuredly not. The giant struggle of the French devolution to promote ideas of liberty and unity, a struggle which was personified in the Emperor Napoleon, has not yet received the final verdict of public opinion. One thunderbolt was not enough to clear the sky. And besides, does not France herself reap the fruits of these stupendous efforts? To what else does she owe, if not to these, the marvellous organization and the powerful unity which make her still the arbiter of the destinies of mankind?

LEONAUR

ALSO FROM LEONAUR
AVAILABLE IN SOFTCOVER OR HARDCOVER WITH DUST JACKET

A HISTORY OF THE FRENCH & INDIAN WAR *by Arthur G. Bradley*—The Seven Years War as it was fought in the New World has always fascinated students of military history—here is the story of that confrontation.

WASHINGTON'S EARLY CAMPAIGNS *by James Hadden*—The French Post Expedition, Great Meadows and Braddock's Defeat—including Braddock's Orderly Books.

BOUQUET & THE OHIO INDIAN WAR *by Cyrus Cort & William Smith*—Two Accounts of the Campaigns of 1763-1764: Bouquet's Campaigns by Cyrus Cort & The History of Bouquet's Expeditions by William Smith.

NARRATIVES OF THE FRENCH & INDIAN WAR: 2 *by David Holden, Samuel Jenks, Lemuel Lyon, Mary Cochrane Rogers & Henry T. Blake*—Contains The Diary of Sergeant David Holden, Captain Samuel Jenks' Journal, The Journal of Lemuel Lyon, Journal of a French Officer at the Siege of Quebec, A Battle Fought on Snowshoes & The Battle of Lake George.

NARRATIVES OF THE FRENCH & INDIAN WAR *by Brown, Eastburn, Hawks & Putnam*—Ranger Brown's Narrative, The Adventures of Robert Eastburn, The Journal of Rufus Putnam—Provincial Infantry & Orderly Book and Journal of Major John Hawks on the Ticonderoga-Crown Point Campaign.

THE 7TH (QUEEN'S OWN) HUSSARS: Volume 1—1688-1792 *by C. R. B. Barrett*—As Dragoons During the Flanders Campaign, War of the Austrian Succession and the Seven Years War.

INDIA'S FREE LANCES *by H. G. Keene*—European Mercenary Commanders in Hindustan 1770-1820.

THE BENGAL EUROPEAN REGIMENT *by P. R. Innes*—An Elite Regiment of the Honourable East India Company 1756-1858.

MUSKET & TOMAHAWK *by Francis Parkman*—A Military History of the French & Indian War, 1753-1760.

THE BLACK WATCH AT TICONDEROGA *by Frederick B. Richards*—Campaigns in the French & Indian War.

QUEEN'S RANGERS *by Frederick B. Richards*—John Simcoe and his Rangers During the Revolutionary War for America.

LEONAUR

ALSO FROM LEONAUR
AVAILABLE IN SOFTCOVER OR HARDCOVER WITH DUST JACKET

THE FALL OF THE MOGHUL EMPIRE OF HINDUSTAN *by H. G. Keene*—By the beginning of the nineteenth century, as British and Indian armies under Lake and Wellesley dominated the scene, a little over half a century of conflict brought the Moghul Empire to its knees.

LADY SALE'S AFGHANISTAN *by Florentia Sale*—An Indomitable Victorian Lady's Account of the Retreat from Kabul During the First Afghan War.

THE CAMPAIGN OF MAGENTA AND SOLFERINO 1859 *by Harold Carmichael Wylly*—The Decisive Conflict for the Unification of Italy.

FRENCH'S CAVALRY CAMPAIGN *by J. G. Maydon*—A Special Correspondent's View of British Army Mounted Troops During the Boer War.

CAVALRY AT WATERLOO *by Sir Evelyn Wood*—British Mounted Troops During the Campaign of 1815.

THE SUBALTERN *by George Robert Gleig*—The Experiences of an Officer of the 85th Light Infantry During the Peninsular War.

NAPOLEON AT BAY, 1814 *by F. Loraine Petre*—The Campaigns to the Fall of the First Empire.

NAPOLEON AND THE CAMPAIGN OF 1806 *by Colonel Vachée*—The Napoleonic Method of Organisation and Command to the Battles of Jena & Auerstädt.

THE COMPLETE ADVENTURES IN THE CONNAUGHT RANGERS *by William Grattan*—The 88th Regiment during the Napoleonic Wars by a Serving Officer.

BUGLER AND OFFICER OF THE RIFLES *by William Green & Harry Smith*—With the 95th (Rifles) during the Peninsular & Waterloo Campaigns of the Napoleonic Wars.

NAPOLEONIC WAR STORIES *by Sir Arthur Quiller-Couch*—Tales of soldiers, spies, battles & sieges from the Peninsular & Waterloo campaingns.

CAPTAIN OF THE 95TH (RIFLES) *by Jonathan Leach*—An officer of Wellington's sharpshooters during the Peninsular, South of France and Waterloo campaigns of the Napoleonic wars.

RIFLEMAN COSTELLO *by Edward Costello*—The adventures of a soldier of the 95th (Rifles) in the Peninsular & Waterloo Campaigns of the Napoleonic wars.

LEONAUR

ALSO FROM LEONAUR
AVAILABLE IN SOFTCOVER OR HARDCOVER WITH DUST JACKET

OFFICERS & GENTLEMEN *by Peter Hawker & William Graham*—Two Accounts of British Officers During the Peninsula War: Officer of Light Dragoons by Peter Hawker & Campaign in Portugal and Spain by William Graham .

THE WALCHEREN EXPEDITION *by Anonymous*—The Experiences of a British Officer of the 81st Regt. During the Campaign in the Low Countries of 1809.

LADIES OF WATERLOO *by Charlotte A. Eaton, Magdalene de Lancey & Juana Smith*—The Experiences of Three Women During the Campaign of 1815: Waterloo Days by Charlotte A. Eaton, A Week at Waterloo by Magdalene de Lancey & Juana's Story by Juana Smith.

JOURNAL OF AN OFFICER IN THE KING'S GERMAN LEGION *by John Frederick Hering*—Recollections of Campaigning During the Napoleonic Wars.

JOURNAL OF AN ARMY SURGEON IN THE PENINSULAR WAR *by Charles Boutflower*—The Recollections of a British Army Medical Man on Campaign During the Napoleonic Wars.

ON CAMPAIGN WITH MOORE AND WELLINGTON *by Anthony Hamilton*—The Experiences of a Soldier of the 43rd Regiment During the Peninsular War.

THE ROAD TO AUSTERLITZ *by R. G. Burton*—Napoleon's Campaign of 1805.

SOLDIERS OF NAPOLEON *by A. J. Doisy De Villargennes & Arthur Chuquet*—The Experiences of the Men of the French First Empire: Under the Eagles by A. J. Doisy De Villargennes & Voices of 1812 by Arthur Chuquet .

INVASION OF FRANCE, 1814 *by F. W. O. Maycock*—The Final Battles of the Napoleonic First Empire.

LEIPZIG—A CONFLICT OF TITANS *by Frederic Shoberl*—A Personal Experience of the 'Battle of the Nations' During the Napoleonic Wars, October 14th-19th, 1813.

SLASHERS *by Charles Cadell*—The Campaigns of the 28th Regiment of Foot During the Napoleonic Wars by a Serving Officer.

BATTLE IMPERIAL *by Charles William Vane*—The Campaigns in Germany & France for the Defeat of Napoleon 1813-1814.

SWIFT & BOLD *by Gibbes Rigaud*—The 60th Rifles During the Peninsula War.

LEONAUR

ALSO FROM LEONAUR

AVAILABLE IN SOFTCOVER OR HARDCOVER WITH DUST JACKET

ADVENTURES OF A YOUNG RIFLEMAN *by Johann Christian Maempel*—The Experiences of a Saxon in the French & British Armies During the Napoleonic Wars.

THE HUSSAR *by Norbert Landsheit & G. R. Gleig*—A German Cavalryman in British Service Throughout the Napoleonic Wars.

RECOLLECTIONS OF THE PENINSULA *by Moyle Sherer*—An Officer of the 34th Regiment of Foot—'The Cumberland Gentlemen'—on Campaign Against Napoleon's French Army in Spain.

MARINE OF REVOLUTION & CONSULATE *by Moreau de Jonnès*—The Recollections of a French Soldier of the Revolutionary Wars 1791-1804.

GENTLEMEN IN RED *by John Dobbs & Robert Knowles*—Two Accounts of British Infantry Officers During the Peninsular War Recollections of an Old 52nd Man by John Dobbs An Officer of Fusiliers by Robert Knowles.

CORPORAL BROWN'S CAMPAIGNS IN THE LOW COUNTRIES *by Robert Brown*—Recollections of a Coldstream Guard in the Early Campaigns Against Revolutionary France 1793-1795.

THE 7TH (QUEENS OWN) HUSSARS: Volume 2—1793-1815 *by C. R. B. Barrett*—During the Campaigns in the Low Countries & the Peninsula and Waterloo Campaigns of the Napoleonic Wars. Volume 2: 1793-1815.

THE MARENGO CAMPAIGN 1800 *by Herbert H. Sargent*—The Victory that Completed the Austrian Defeat in Italy.

DONALDSON OF THE 94TH—SCOTS BRIGADE *by Joseph Donaldson*—The Recollections of a Soldier During the Peninsula & South of France Campaigns of the Napoleonic Wars.

A CONSCRIPT FOR EMPIRE *by Philippe as told to Johann Christian Maempel*—The Experiences of a Young German Conscript During the Napoleonic Wars.

JOURNAL OF THE CAMPAIGN OF 1815 *by Alexander Cavalié Mercer*—The Experiences of an Officer of the Royal Horse Artillery During the Waterloo Campaign.

NAPOLEON'S CAMPAIGNS IN POLAND 1806-7 *by Robert Wilson*—The campaign in Poland from the Russian side of the conflict.

LEONAUR

ALSO FROM LEONAUR
AVAILABLE IN SOFTCOVER OR HARDCOVER WITH DUST JACKET

OMPTEDA OF THE KING'S GERMAN LEGION *by Christian von Ompteda*—A Hanoverian Officer on Campaign Against Napoleon.

LIEUTENANT SIMMONS OF THE 95TH (RIFLES) *by George Simmons*—Recollections of the Peninsula, South of France & Waterloo Campaigns of the Napoleonic Wars.

A HORSEMAN FOR THE EMPEROR *by Jean Baptiste Gazzola*—A Cavalryman of Napoleon's Army on Campaign Throughout the Napoleonic Wars.

SERGEANT LAWRENCE *by William Lawrence*—With the 40th Regt. of Foot in South America, the Peninsular War & at Waterloo.

CAMPAIGNS WITH THE FIELD TRAIN *by Richard D. Henegan*—Experiences of a British Officer During the Peninsula and Waterloo Campaigns of the Napoleonic Wars.

CAVALRY SURGEON *by S. D. Broughton*—On Campaign Against Napoleon in the Peninsula & South of France During the Napoleonic Wars 1812-1814.

MEN OF THE RIFLES *by Thomas Knight, Henry Curling & Jonathan Leach*—The Reminiscences of Thomas Knight of the 95th (Rifles) by Thomas Knight, Henry Curling's Anecdotes by Henry Curling & The Field Services of the Rifle Brigade from its Formation to Waterloo by Jonathan Leach.

THE ULM CAMPAIGN 1805 *by F. N. Maude*—Napoleon and the Defeat of the Austrian Army During the 'War of the Third Coalition'.

SOLDIERING WITH THE 'DIVISION' *by Thomas Garrety*—The Military Experiences of an Infantryman of the 43rd Regiment During the Napoleonic Wars.

SERGEANT MORRIS OF THE 73RD FOOT *by Thomas Morris*—The Experiences of a British Infantryman During the Napoleonic Wars-Including Campaigns in Germany and at Waterloo.

A VOICE FROM WATERLOO *by Edward Cotton*—The Personal Experiences of a British Cavalryman Who Became a Battlefield Guide and Authority on the Campaign of 1815.

NAPOLEON AND HIS MARSHALS *by J. T. Headley*—The Men of the First Empire.

LEONAUR

ALSO FROM LEONAUR

AVAILABLE IN SOFTCOVER OR HARDCOVER WITH DUST JACKET

COLBORNE: A SINGULAR TALENT FOR WAR *by John Colborne*—The Napoleonic Wars Career of One of Wellington's Most Highly Valued Officers in Egypt, Holland, Italy, the Peninsula and at Waterloo.

NAPOLEON'S RUSSIAN CAMPAIGN *by Philippe Henri de Segur*—The Invasion, Battles and Retreat by an Aide-de-Camp on the Emperor's Staff.

WITH THE LIGHT DIVISION *by John H. Cooke*—The Experiences of an Officer of the 43rd Light Infantry in the Peninsula and South of France During the Napoleonic Wars.

WELLINGTON AND THE PYRENEES CAMPAIGN VOLUME I: FROM VITORIA TO THE BIDASSOA *by F. C. Beatson*—The final phase of the campaign in the Iberian Peninsula.

WELLINGTON AND THE INVASION OF FRANCE VOLUME II: THE BIDASSOA TO THE BATTLE OF THE NIVELLE *by F. C. Beatson*—The final phase of the campaign in the Iberian Peninsula.

WELLINGTON AND THE FALL OF FRANCE VOLUME III: THE GAVES AND THE BATTLE OF ORTHEZ *by F. C. Beatson*—The final phase of the campaign in the Iberian Peninsula.

NAPOLEON'S IMPERIAL GUARD: FROM MARENGO TO WATERLOO *by J. T. Headley*—The story of Napoleon's Imperial Guard and the men who commanded them.

BATTLES & SIEGES OF THE PENINSULAR WAR *by W. H. Fitchett*—Corunna, Busaco, Albuera, Ciudad Rodrigo, Badajos, Salamanca, San Sebastian & Others.

SERGEANT GUILLEMARD: THE MAN WHO SHOT NELSON? *by Robert Guillemard*—A Soldier of the Infantry of the French Army of Napoleon on Campaign Throughout Europe.

WITH THE GUARDS ACROSS THE PYRENEES *by Robert Batty*—The Experiences of a British Officer of Wellington's Army During the Battles for the Fall of Napoleonic France, 1813 .

A STAFF OFFICER IN THE PENINSULA *by E. W. Buckham*—An Officer of the British Staff Corps Cavalry During the Peninsula Campaign of the Napoleonic Wars.

THE LEIPZIG CAMPAIGN: 1813—NAPOLEON AND THE "BATTLE OF THE NATIONS" *by F. N. Maude*—Colonel Maude's analysis of Napoleon's campaign of 1813 around Leipzig.

LEONAUR

ALSO FROM LEONAUR
AVAILABLE IN SOFTCOVER OR HARDCOVER WITH DUST JACKET

CAPTAIN COIGNET *by Jean-Roch Coignet*—A Soldier of Napoleon's Imperial Guard from the Italian Campaign to Russia and Waterloo.

HUSSAR ROCCA *by Albert Jean Michel de Rocca*—A French cavalry officer's experiences of the Napoleonic Wars and his views on the Peninsular Campaigns against the Spanish, British And Guerilla Armies.

MARINES TO 95TH (RIFLES) *by Thomas Fernyhough*—The military experiences of Robert Fernyhough during the Napoleonic Wars.

LIGHT BOB *by Robert Blakeney*—The experiences of a young officer in H.M 28th & 36th regiments of the British Infantry during the Peninsular Campaign of the Napoleonic Wars 1804 - 1814.

WITH WELLINGTON'S LIGHT CAVALRY *by William Tomkinson*—The Experiences of an officer of the 16th Light Dragoons in the Peninsular and Waterloo campaigns of the Napoleonic Wars.

SERGEANT BOURGOGNE *by Adrien Bourgogne*—With Napoleon's Imperial Guard in the Russian Campaign and on the Retreat from Moscow 1812 - 13.

SURTEES OF THE 95TH (RIFLES) *by William Surtees*—A Soldier of the 95th (Rifles) in the Peninsular campaign of the Napoleonic Wars.

SWORDS OF HONOUR *by Henry Newbolt & Stanley L. Wood*—The Careers of Six Outstanding Officers from the Napoleonic Wars, the Wars for India and the American Civil War.

ENSIGN BELL IN THE PENINSULAR WAR *by George Bell*—The Experiences of a young British Soldier of the 34th Regiment 'The Cumberland Gentlemen' in the Napoleonic wars.

HUSSAR IN WINTER *by Alexander Gordon*—A British Cavalry Officer during the retreat to Corunna in the Peninsular campaign of the Napoleonic Wars.

THE COMPLEAT RIFLEMAN HARRIS *by Benjamin Harris as told to and transcribed by Captain Henry Curling, 52nd Regt. of Foot*—The adventures of a soldier of the 95th (Rifles) during the Peninsular Campaign of the Napoleonic Wars.

THE ADVENTURES OF A LIGHT DRAGOON *by George Farmer & G.R. Gleig*—A cavalryman during the Peninsular & Waterloo Campaigns, in captivity & at the siege of Bhurtpore, India.

LEONAUR

ALSO FROM LEONAUR
AVAILABLE IN SOFTCOVER OR HARDCOVER WITH DUST JACKET

THE LIFE OF THE REAL BRIGADIER GERARD VOLUME 1—THE YOUNG HUSSAR 1782-1807 *by Jean-Baptiste De Marbot*—A French Cavalryman Of the Napoleonic Wars at Marengo, Austerlitz, Jena, Eylau & Friedland.

THE LIFE OF THE REAL BRIGADIER GERARD VOLUME 2—IMPERIAL AIDE-DE-CAMP 1807-1811 *by Jean-Baptiste De Marbot*—A French Cavalryman of the Napoleonic Wars at Saragossa, Landshut, Eckmuhl, Ratisbon, Aspern-Essling, Wagram, Busaco & Torres Vedras.

THE LIFE OF THE REAL BRIGADIER GERARD VOLUME 3—COLONEL OF CHASSEURS 1811-1815 *by Jean-Baptiste De Marbot*—A French Cavalryman in the retreat from Moscow, Lutzen, Bautzen, Katzbach, Leipzig, Hanau & Waterloo.

THE INDIAN WAR OF 1864 *by Eugene Ware*—The Experiences of a Young Officer of the 7th Iowa Cavalry on the Western Frontier During the Civil War.

THE MARCH OF DESTINY *by Charles E. Young & V. Devinny*—Dangers of the Trail in 1865 by Charles E. Young & The Story of a Pioneer by V. Devinny, two Accounts of Early Emigrants to Colorado.

CROSSING THE PLAINS *by William Audley Maxwell*—A First Hand Narrative of the Early Pioneer Trail to California in 1857.

CHIEF OF SCOUTS *by William F. Drannan*—A Pilot to Emigrant and Government Trains, Across the Plains of the Western Frontier.

THIRTY-ONE YEARS ON THE PLAINS AND IN THE MOUNTAINS *by William F. Drannan*—William Drannan was born to be a pioneer, hunter, trapper and wagon train guide during the momentous days of the Great American West.

THE INDIAN WARS VOLUNTEER *by William Thompson*—Recollections of the Conflict Against the Snakes, Shoshone, Bannocks, Modocs and Other Native Tribes of the American North West.

THE 4TH TENNESSEE CAVALRY *by George B. Guild*—The Services of Smith's Regiment of Confederate Cavalry by One of its Officers.

COLONEL WORTHINGTON'S SHILOH *by T. Worthington*—The Tennessee Campaign, 1862, by an Officer of the Ohio Volunteers.

FOUR YEARS IN THE SADDLE *by W. L. Curry*—The History of the First Regiment Ohio Volunteer Cavalry in the American Civil War.

LEONAUR

ALSO FROM LEONAUR
AVAILABLE IN SOFTCOVER OR HARDCOVER WITH DUST JACKET

ESCAPE FROM THE FRENCH *by Edward Boys*—A Young Royal Navy Midshipman's Adventures During the Napoleonic War.

THE VOYAGE OF H.M.S. PANDORA *by Edward Edwards R. N. & George Hamilton, edited by Basil Thomson*—In Pursuit of the Mutineers of the Bounty in the South Seas—1790-1791.

MEDUSA *by J. B. Henry Savigny and Alexander Correard and Charlotte-Adélaïde Dard* —Narrative of a Voyage to Senegal in 1816 & The Sufferings of the Picard Family After the Shipwreck of the Medusa.

THE SEA WAR OF 1812 VOLUME 1 *by A. T. Mahan*—A History of the Maritime Conflict.

THE SEA WAR OF 1812 VOLUME 2 *by A. T. Mahan*—A History of the Maritime Conflict.

WETHERELL OF H. M. S. HUSSAR *by John Wetherell*—The Recollections of an Ordinary Seaman of the Royal Navy During the Napoleonic Wars.

THE NAVAL BRIGADE IN NATAL *by C. R. N. Burne*—With the Guns of H. M. S. Terrible & H. M. S. Tartar during the Boer War 1899-1900.

THE VOYAGE OF H. M. S. BOUNTY *by William Bligh*—The True Story of an 18th Century Voyage of Exploration and Mutiny.

SHIPWRECK! *by William Gilly*—The Royal Navy's Disasters at Sea 1793-1849.

KING'S CUTTERS AND SMUGGLERS: 1700-1855 *by E. Keble Chatterton*—A unique period of maritime history-from the beginning of the eighteenth to the middle of the nineteenth century when British seamen risked all to smuggle valuable goods from wool to tea and spirits from and to the Continent.

CONFEDERATE BLOCKADE RUNNER *by John Wilkinson*—The Personal Recollections of an Officer of the Confederate Navy.

NAVAL BATTLES OF THE NAPOLEONIC WARS *by W. H. Fitchett*—Cape St. Vincent, the Nile, Cadiz, Copenhagen, Trafalgar & Others.

PRISONERS OF THE RED DESERT *by R. S. Gwatkin-Williams*—The Adventures of the Crew of the Tara During the First World War.

U-BOAT WAR 1914-1918 *by James B. Connolly/Karl von Schenk*—Two Contrasting Accounts from Both Sides of the Conflict at Sea D uring the Great War.

LEONAUR

ALSO FROM LEONAUR
AVAILABLE IN SOFTCOVER OR HARDCOVER WITH DUST JACKET

IRON TIMES WITH THE GUARDS *by An O. E. (G. P. A. Fildes)*—The Experiences of an Officer of the Coldstream Guards on the Western Front During the First World War.

THE GREAT WAR IN THE MIDDLE EAST: 1 *by W. T. Massey*—The Desert Campaigns & How Jerusalem Was Won---two classic accounts in one volume.

THE GREAT WAR IN THE MIDDLE EAST: 2 *by W. T. Massey*—Allenby's Final Triumph.

SMITH-DORRIEN *by Horace Smith-Dorrien*—Isandlwhana to the Great War.

1914 *by Sir John French*—The Early Campaigns of the Great War by the British Commander.

GRENADIER *by E. R. M. Fryer*—The Recollections of an Officer of the Grenadier Guards throughout the Great War on the Western Front.

BATTLE, CAPTURE & ESCAPE *by George Pearson*—The Experiences of a Canadian Light Infantryman During the Great War.

DIGGERS AT WAR *by R. Hugh Knyvett & G. P. Cuttriss*—"Over There" With the Australians by R. Hugh Knyvett and Over the Top With the Third Australian Division by G. P. Cuttriss. Accounts of Australians During the Great War in the Middle East, at Gallipoli and on the Western Front.

HEAVY FIGHTING BEFORE US *by George Brenton Laurie*—The Letters of an Officer of the Royal Irish Rifles on the Western Front During the Great War.

THE CAMELIERS *by Oliver Hogue*—A Classic Account of the Australians of the Imperial Camel Corps During the First World War in the Middle East.

RED DUST *by Donald Black*—A Classic Account of Australian Light Horsemen in Palestine During the First World War.

THE LEAN, BROWN MEN *by Angus Buchanan*—Experiences in East Africa During the Great War with the 25th Royal Fusiliers—the Legion of Frontiersmen.

THE NIGERIAN REGIMENT IN EAST AFRICA *by W. D. Downes*—On Campaign During the Great War 1916-1918.

THE 'DIE-HARDS' IN SIBERIA *by John Ward*—With the Middlesex Regiment Against the Bolsheviks 1918-19.

LEONAUR

ALSO FROM LEONAUR
AVAILABLE IN SOFTCOVER OR HARDCOVER WITH DUST JACKET

FARAWAY CAMPAIGN *by F. James*—Experiences of an Indian Army Cavalry Officer in Persia & Russia During the Great War.

REVOLT IN THE DESERT *by T. E. Lawrence*—An account of the experiences of one remarkable British officer's war from his own perspective.

MACHINE-GUN SQUADRON *by A. M. G.*—The 20th Machine Gunners from British Yeomanry Regiments in the Middle East Campaign of the First World War.

A GUNNER'S CRUSADE *by Antony Bluett*—The Campaign in the Desert, Palestine & Syria as Experienced by the Honourable Artillery Company During the Great War .

DESPATCH RIDER *by W. H. L. Watson*—The Experiences of a British Army Motorcycle Despatch Rider During the Opening Battles of the Great War in Europe.

TIGERS ALONG THE TIGRIS *by E. J. Thompson*—The Leicestershire Regiment in Mesopotamia During the First World War.

HEARTS & DRAGONS *by Charles R. M. F. Crutwell*—The 4th Royal Berkshire Regiment in France and Italy During the Great War, 1914-1918.

INFANTRY BRIGADE: 1914 *by John Ward*—The Diary of a Commander of the 15th Infantry Brigade, 5th Division, British Army, During the Retreat from Mons.

DOING OUR 'BIT' *by Ian Hay*—Two Classic Accounts of the Men of Kitchener's 'New Army' During the Great War including *The First 100,000 & All In It*.

AN EYE IN THE STORM *by Arthur Ruhl*—An American War Correspondent's Experiences of the First World War from the Western Front to Gallipoli-and Beyond.

STAND & FALL *by Joe Cassells*—With the Middlesex Regiment Against the Bolsheviks 1918-19.

RIFLEMAN MACGILL'S WAR *by Patrick MacGill*—A Soldier of the London Irish During the Great War in Europe including *The Amateur Army, The Red Horizon & The Great Push*.

WITH THE GUNS *by C. A. Rose & Hugh Dalton*—Two First Hand Accounts of British Gunners at War in Europe During World War 1- Three Years in France with the Guns and With the British Guns in Italy.

THE BUSH WAR DOCTOR *by Robert V. Dolbey*—The Experiences of a British Army Doctor During the East African Campaign of the First World War.

Lightning Source UK Ltd.
Milton Keynes UK
UKOW05f2235250614

234069UK00001B/42/P

9 781782 822325